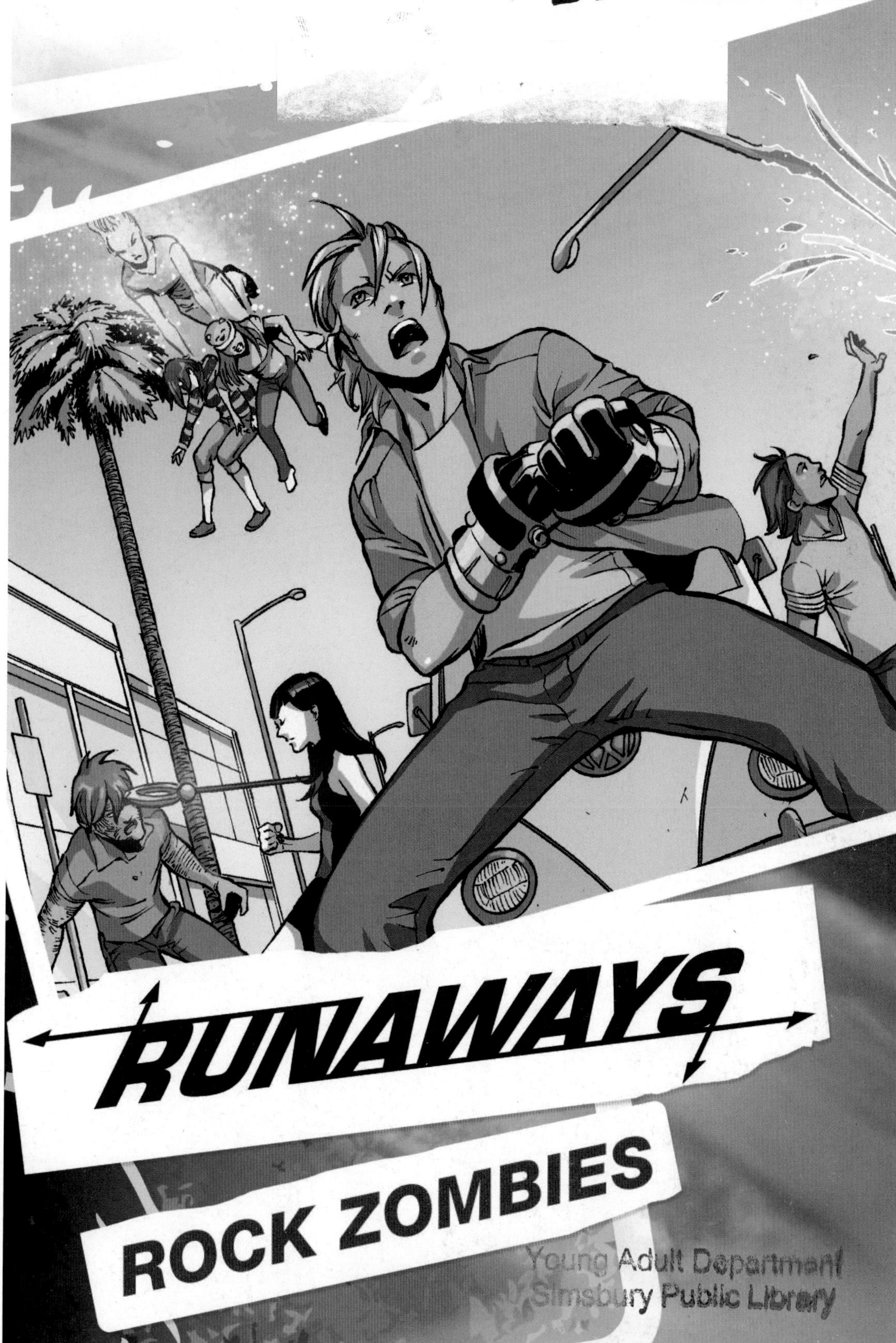

# RUNAWAYS

## ROCK ZOMBIES

# RUNAWAYS

## ROCK ZOMBIES

WRITER: **TERRY MOORE**

PENCILER: **TAKESHI MIYAZAWA**

INKERS: **TAKESHI MIYAZAWA, NORMAN LEE &**
**CRAIG YEUNG**

COVER ART: **HUMBERTO RAMOS** & **CHRISTINA STRAIN**

"MOLLIFEST DESTINY"
WRITER: **CHRIS YOST**
ARTIST: **SARA PICHELLI**

"TRUTH OR DARE"
WRITER: **JAMES ASMUS**
ARTIST: **EMMA RIOS**
COVER ART: **DAVID LAFUENTE** & **CHRISTINA STRAIN**

COLORIST: **CHRISTINA STRAIN**
LETTERER: **VC'S JOE CARAMAGNA**
EDITORS: **NICK LOWE** & **DANIEL KETCHUM**

RUNAWAYS CREATED BY **BRIAN K. VAUGHAN** & **ADRIAN ALPHONA**

COLLECTION EDITOR: **JENNIFER GRÜNWALD**
EDITORIAL ASSISTANT: **ALEX STARBUCK**
ASSISTANT EDITORS: **CORY LEVINE** & **JOHN DENNING**
EDITOR, SPECIAL PROJECTS: **MARK D. BEAZLEY**
SENIOR EDITOR, SPECIAL PROJECTS: **JEFF YOUNGQUIST**
SENIOR VICE PRESIDENT OF SALES: **DAVID GABRIEL**

EDITOR IN CHIEF: **JOE QUESADA**
PUBLISHER: **DAN BUCKLEY**
EXECUTIVE PRODUCER: **ALAN FINE**

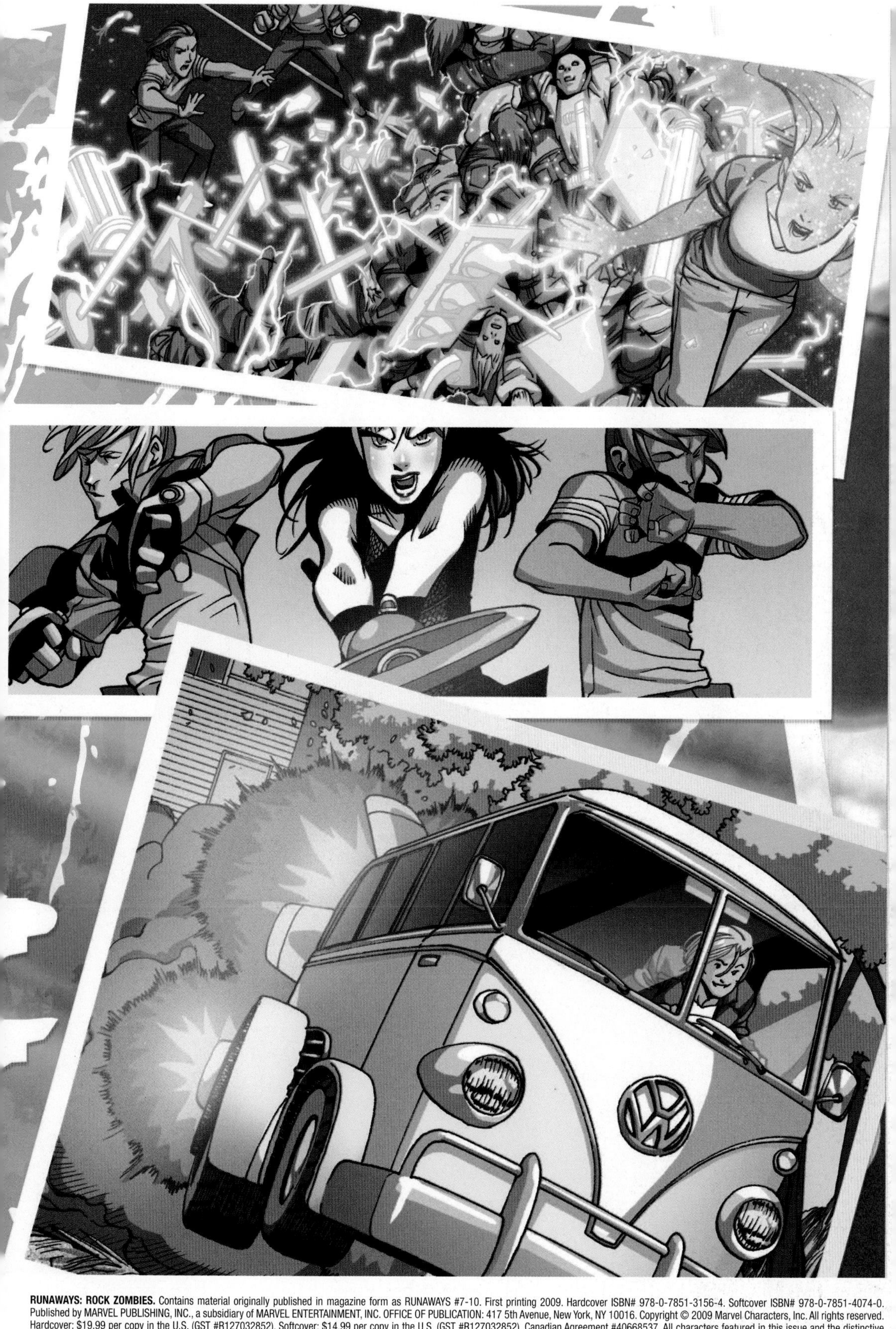

**RUNAWAYS: ROCK ZOMBIES.** Contains material originally published in magazine form as RUNAWAYS #7-10. First printing 2009. Hardcover ISBN# 978-0-7851-3156-4. Softcover ISBN# 978-0-7851-4074-0. Published by MARVEL PUBLISHING, INC., a subsidiary of MARVEL ENTERTAINMENT, INC. OFFICE OF PUBLICATION: 417 5th Avenue, New York, NY 10016.  Hardcover: $19.99 per copy in the U.S. (GST #R127032852). Softcover: $14.99 per copy in the U.S. (GST #R127032852). Canadian Agreement #40668537.  **Printed in the U.S.A.** ALAN FINE, CEO Marvel Publishing Division and EVP & CMO Marvel Characters B.V.; DAN BUCKLEY, President of Publishing - Print & Digital Media; JIM SOKOLOWSKI, Chief Operating Officer; DAVID GABRIEL, SVP of Publishing Sales & Circulation; DAVID BOGART, SVP of Business Affairs & Talent Management; MICHAEL PASCIULLO, VP Merchandising & Communications; JIM O'KEEFE, VP of Operations & Logistics; DAN CARR, Executive Director of Publishing Technology; JUSTIN F. GABRIE, Director of Publishing & Editorial Operations; SUSAN CRESPI, Editorial Operations Manager; ALEX MORALES, Publishing Operations Manager; STAN LEE, Chairman Emeritus. For information regarding advertising in Marvel Comics or on Marvel.com, please contact Mitch Dane, Advertising Director, at mdane@marvel.com. For Marvel subscription inquiries, please call 800-217-9158.

10 9 8 7 6 5 4 3 2 1

# PREVIOUSLY

AT SOME POINT IN THEIR LIVES, ALL KIDS THINK THAT THEIR PARENTS ARE EVIL. FOR MOLLY HAYES AND HER FRIENDS, THIS IS ESPECIALLY TRUE. ONE NIGHT, MOLLY AND HER FRIENDS DISCOVERED THAT THEIR PARENTS WERE A GROUP OF SUPER-POWERED CRIME BOSSES WHO CALLED THEMSELVES "THE PRIDE." USING TECHNOLOGY AND RESOURCES STOLEN FROM THEIR PARENTS, THE TEENAGERS WERE ABLE TO STOP THE PRIDE AND BREAK THEIR CRIMINAL HOLD ON LOS ANGELES. BUT THEY'VE BEEN ON THE RUN EVER SINCE.

ATTACKED BY A CREW OF MAJESDANIAN SOLDIERS INTENT ON CAPTURING THE RUNAWAYS' KAROLINA DEAN—WHOM THEY HOLD RESPONSIBLE FOR THE DESTRUCTION OF THEIR HOME PLANET—THE RUNAWAYS FIGHT BACK AND DO EVERYTHING THEY CAN TO ESCAPE. BUT WHEN THEY REALIZE THAT THIS IS A FIGHT THEY WON'T BE ABLE TO WIN, THE SHAPESHIFTING XAVIN TAKES KAROLINA'S PLACE AND WILLINGLY AGREES TO GO WITH THE MAJESDANIANS, LEAVING HER FELLOW RUNAWAYS BEHIND.

Man, and I thought I was noisy. Sounds like Godzilla attacking a kindergarten down here.

Why won't you dieeee?!

Never!

Oh, good morning, Chase. How are you? I'm fine, thanks. Where are you going? Have to go to work, kids, put food on the table and game controllers in your hands. Oh, thank you, Chase. Thank you from the bottom of our wee little hearts.

AAIIEEGH!

Ha ha!

Don't wait up. I may stop off at the club and have a drink with the boys. Bye, Chase! Hurry back.

I win! I win! I love cheating!

Protest! I wanna see the instant replay!

You guys play too rough!

Every once in a while, it will hit me.

What?

This. All This. Everything.

There goes Chase, off to work. What a surprise, huh?

I know, I can't believe he's sticking with it.

Talk about an eco footprint... that crazy Stein bus he's driving now...

WREEEGH...

CHING-GA! CLANG!

VRROOOOM!

Chase, you freakin' ape! Way to stay under the radar, genius!

‹sigh›

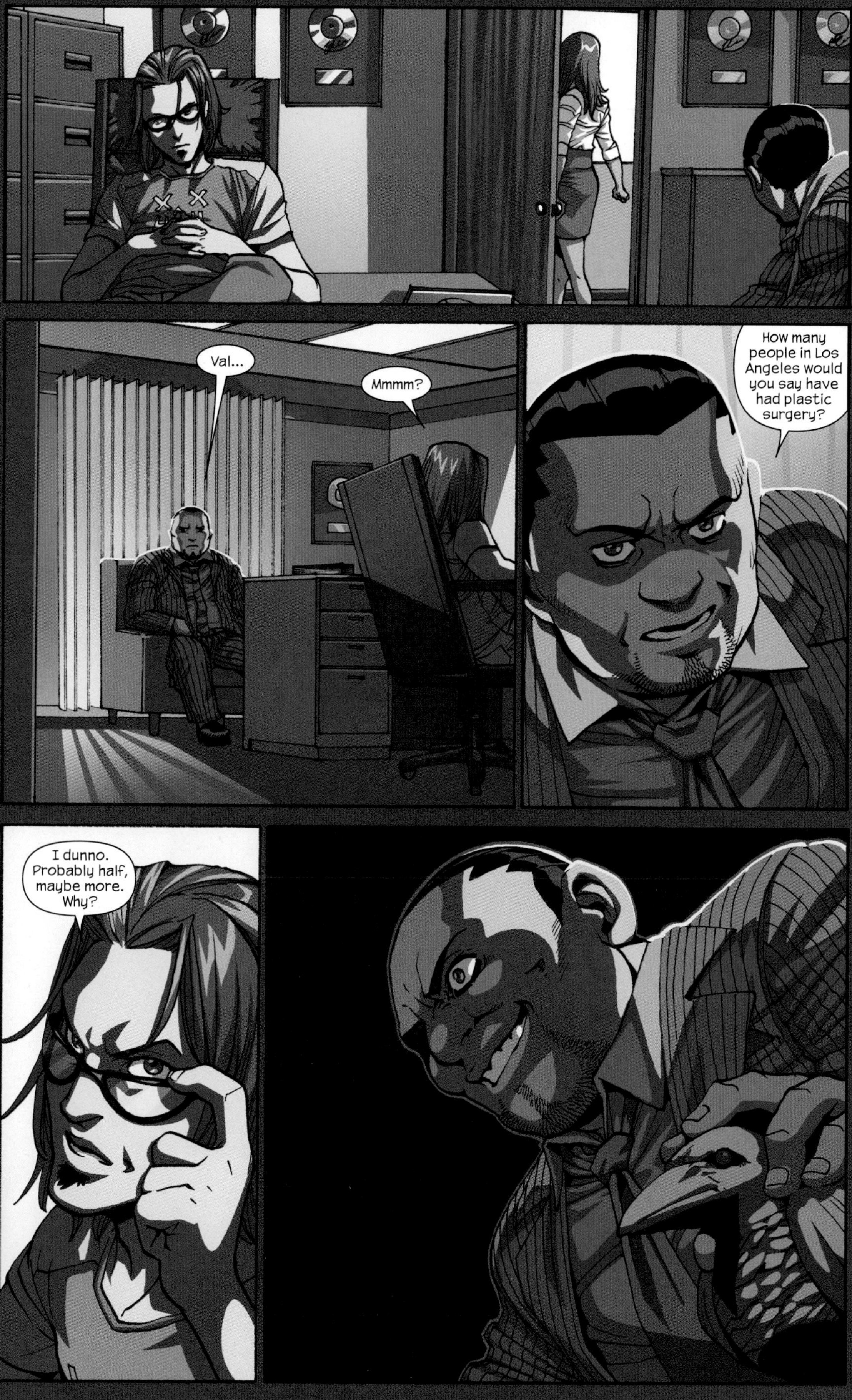

Val...
Mmmm?
How many people in Los Angeles would you say have had plastic surgery?
I dunno. Probably half, maybe more. Why?

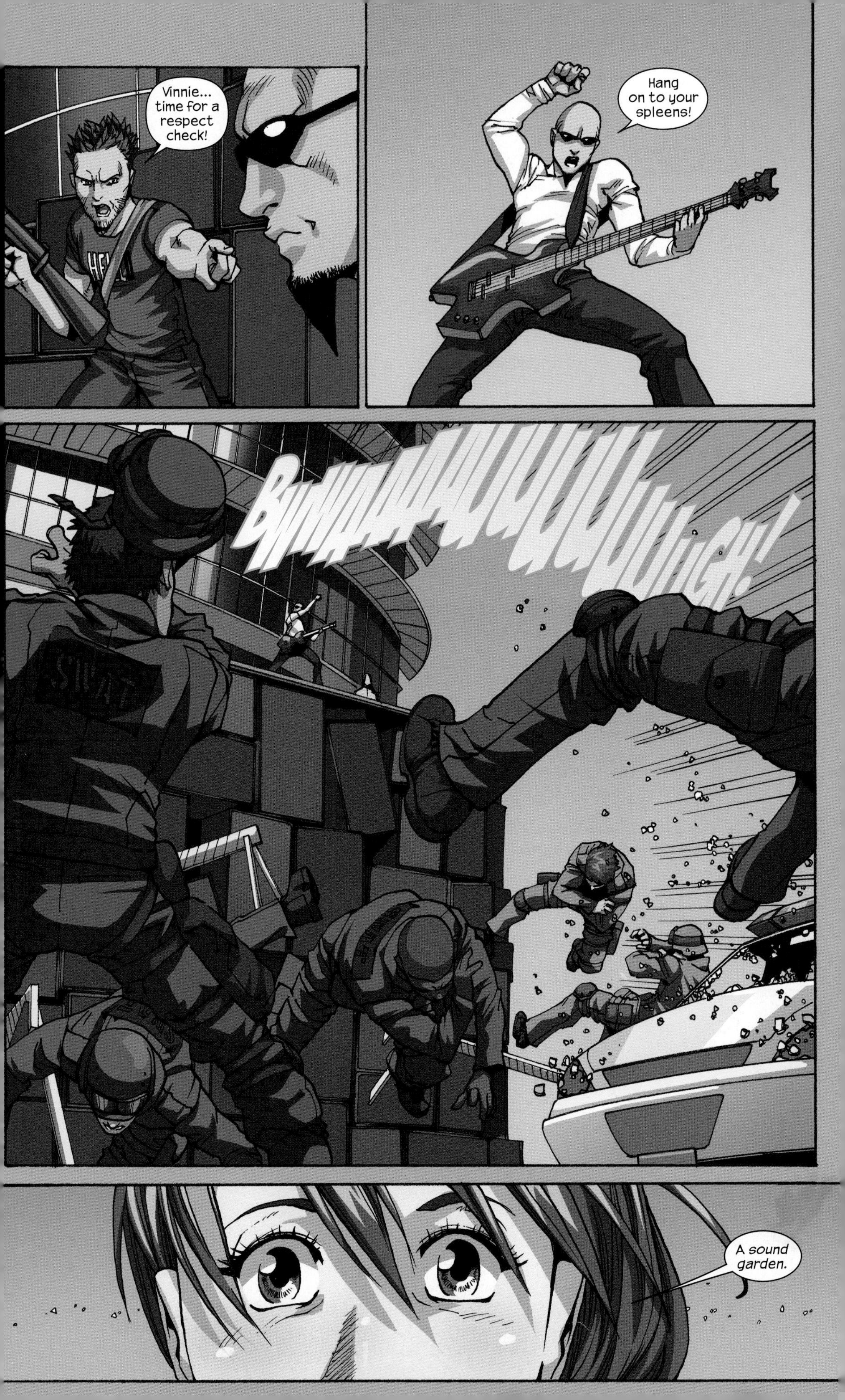
Vinnie... time for a respect check!
Hang on to your spleens!
BWNAAAAUUUUUUUUUGH!
A sound garden.

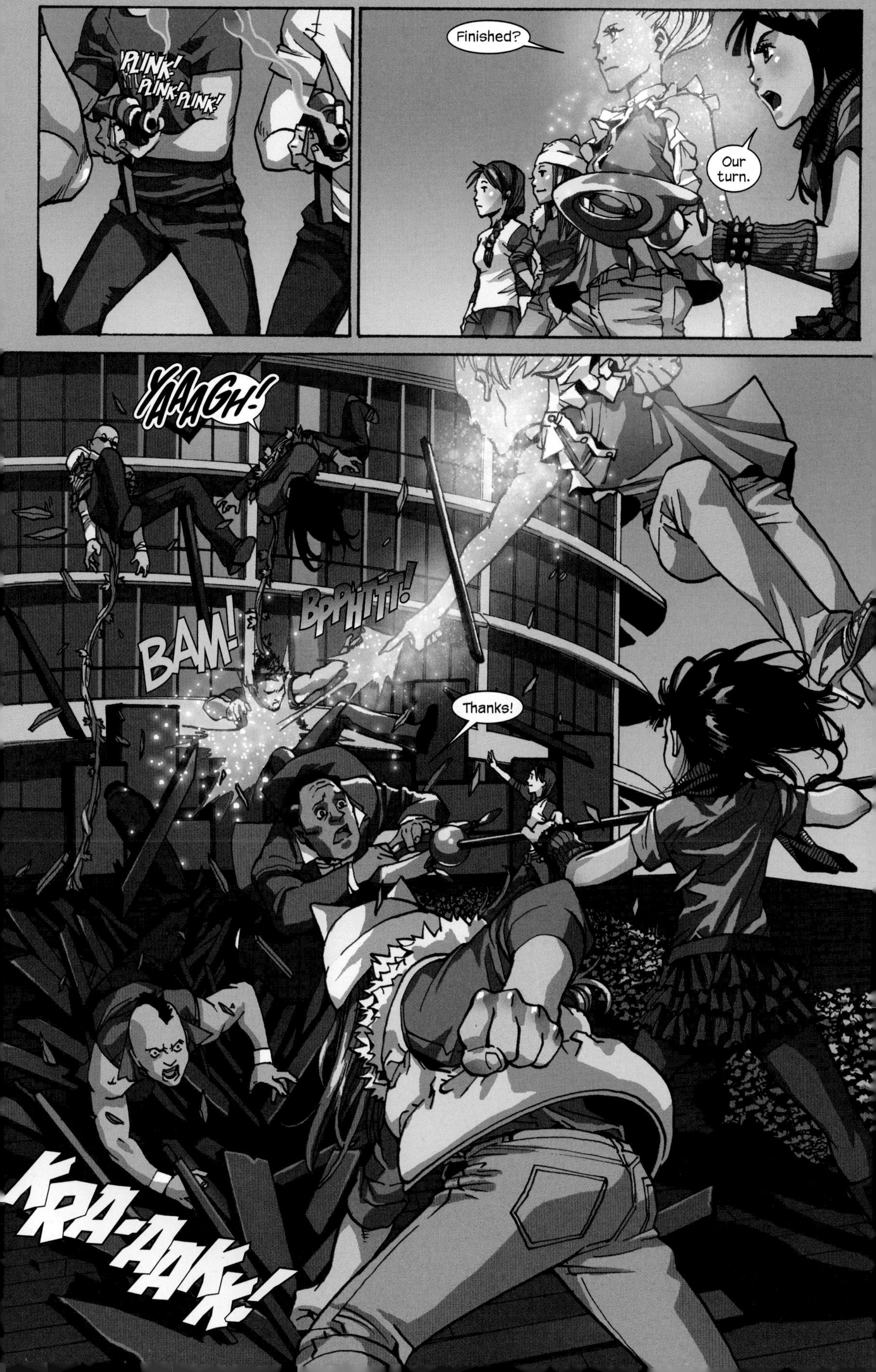
PLINK! PLINK! PLINK! PLINK!
Finished?
Our turn.
YAAAGH!
BAM!
BPPHTTT!
Thanks!
KRA-AAKK!

SWAT One, what the hell is goin' on up there?!

You wouldn't believe me if I told you, captain. Uh...threat neutralized.

Oh great, I barely get the frog parked and you guys are already finished.

Well, not exactly fighting the cream of the crop here, are we?

Okay, we need to get out of here before somebody starts asking questions...like who's going to pay for this mess.

Oh. Right.

There. Just because they're prisoners doesn't mean they can't look pretty.

You missed a spot.

Molly, Klara...let's go.

You! Hit the deck!

We kind of already did that. Bye!

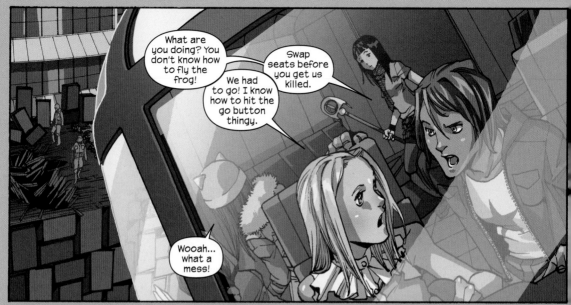

What are you doing? You don't know how to fly the frog!

Swap seats before you get us killed.

We had to go! I know how to hit the go button thingy.

Wooah... what a mess!

So, what do you think?

Good execution, nice teamwork. In and out. I think we're ready to get back to the big time. There's just one problem.

What?

Chase.

Mail call.

Thank you, Chase. Just leave it there.

Lydia, I hold in my hand the next big hit, and nobody has it but KZIT and yours truly!

Way to go, Val! Who is it?

Just a little electronic dance rap I knocked out on Garage Band...with a little something extra added in. See what you think.

Nice beat.

Turn it up.

What do you think?

I like it! What's that chanting in the background?

What?

I like it. Great dance beat.

Then let's dance! C'mon.

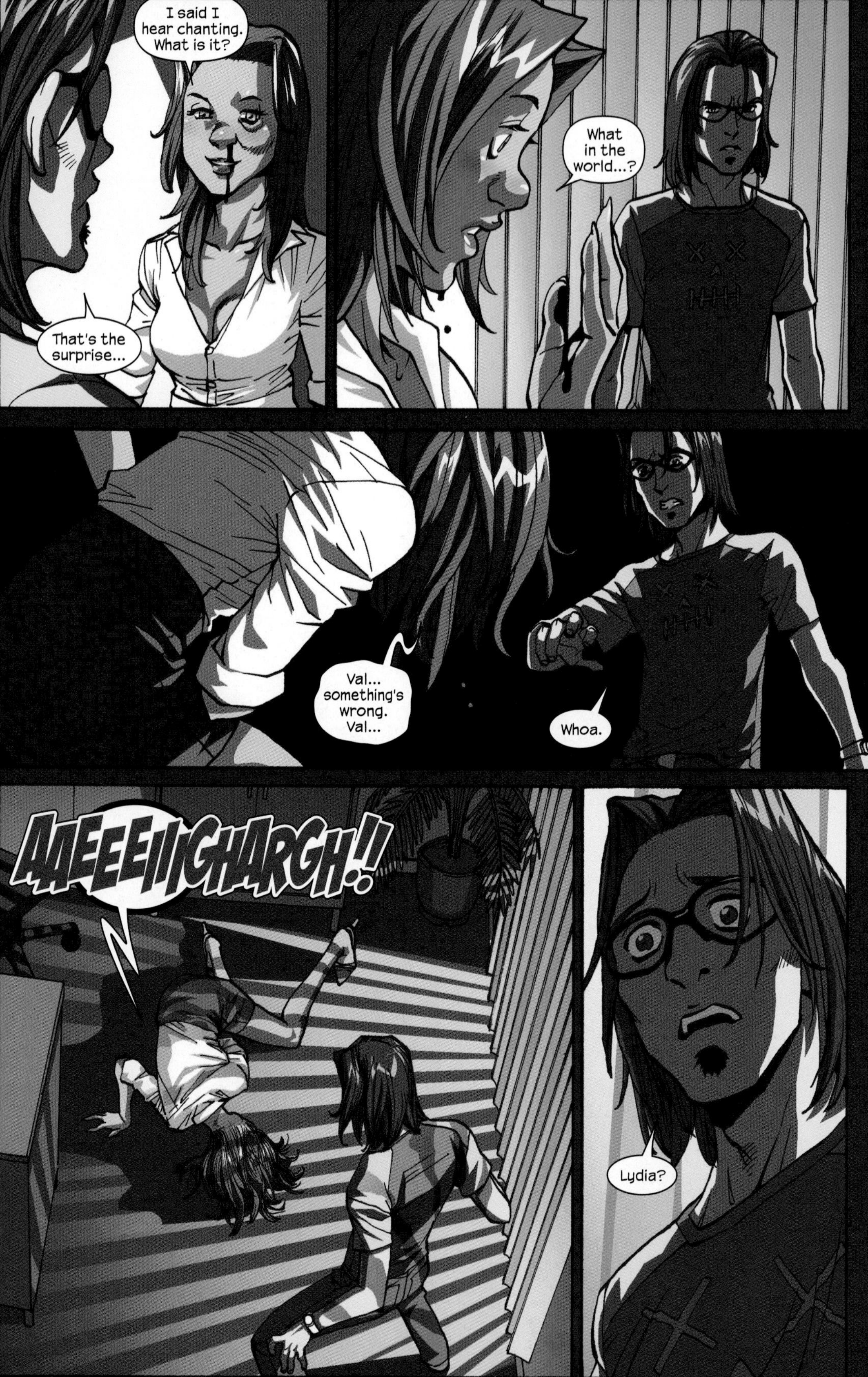
I said I hear chanting. What is it?
That's the surprise...
What in the world...?
Val... something's wrong. Val...
Whoa.
AAEEEIIIGHARGH!!
Lydia?

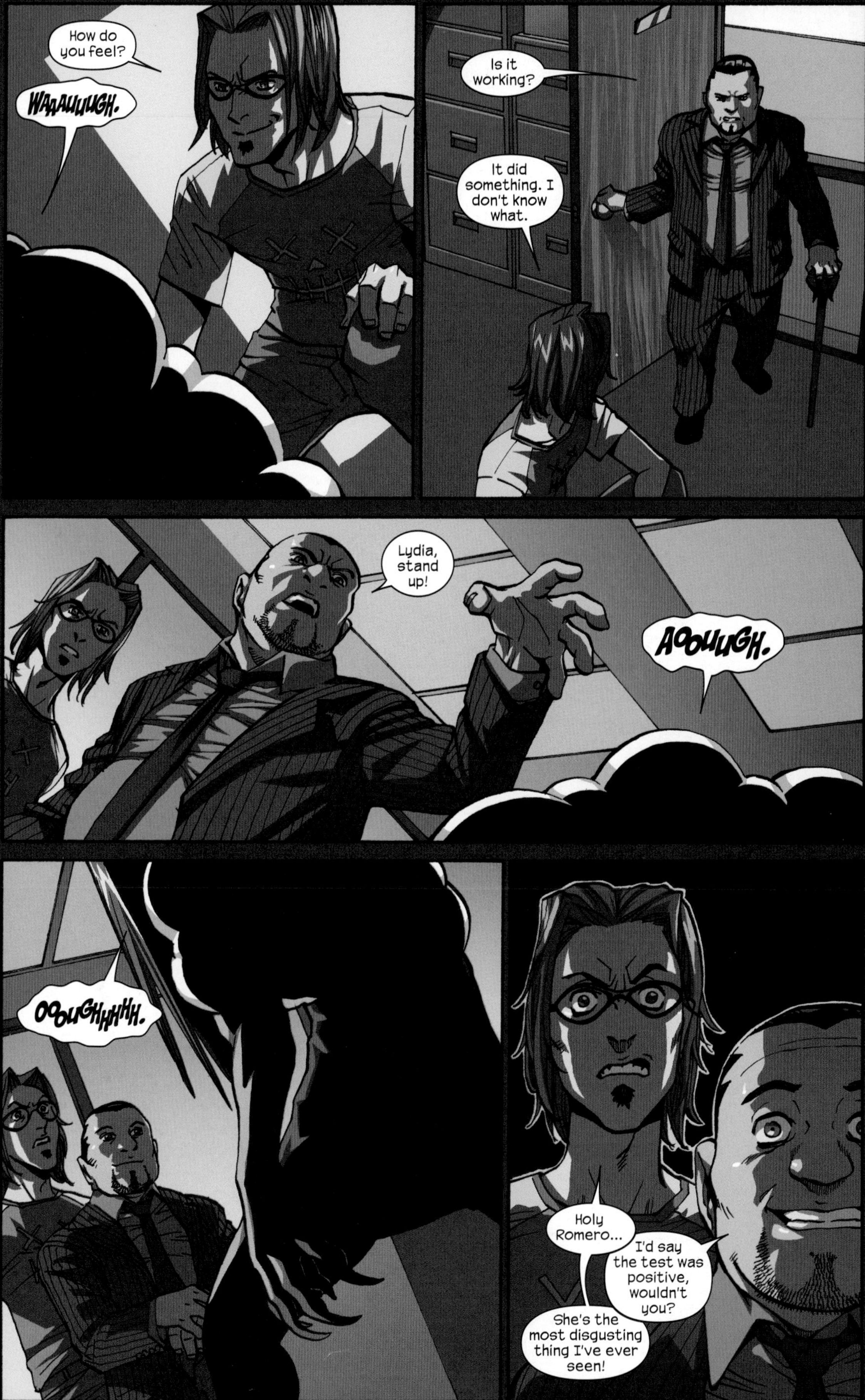
How do you feel?
WAAAUUUGH.
Is it working?
It did something. I don't know what.
Lydia, stand up!
AOOUUGH.
OOOUGHHHHH.
Holy Romero...
I'd say the test was positive, wouldn't you?
She's the most disgusting thing I've ever seen!

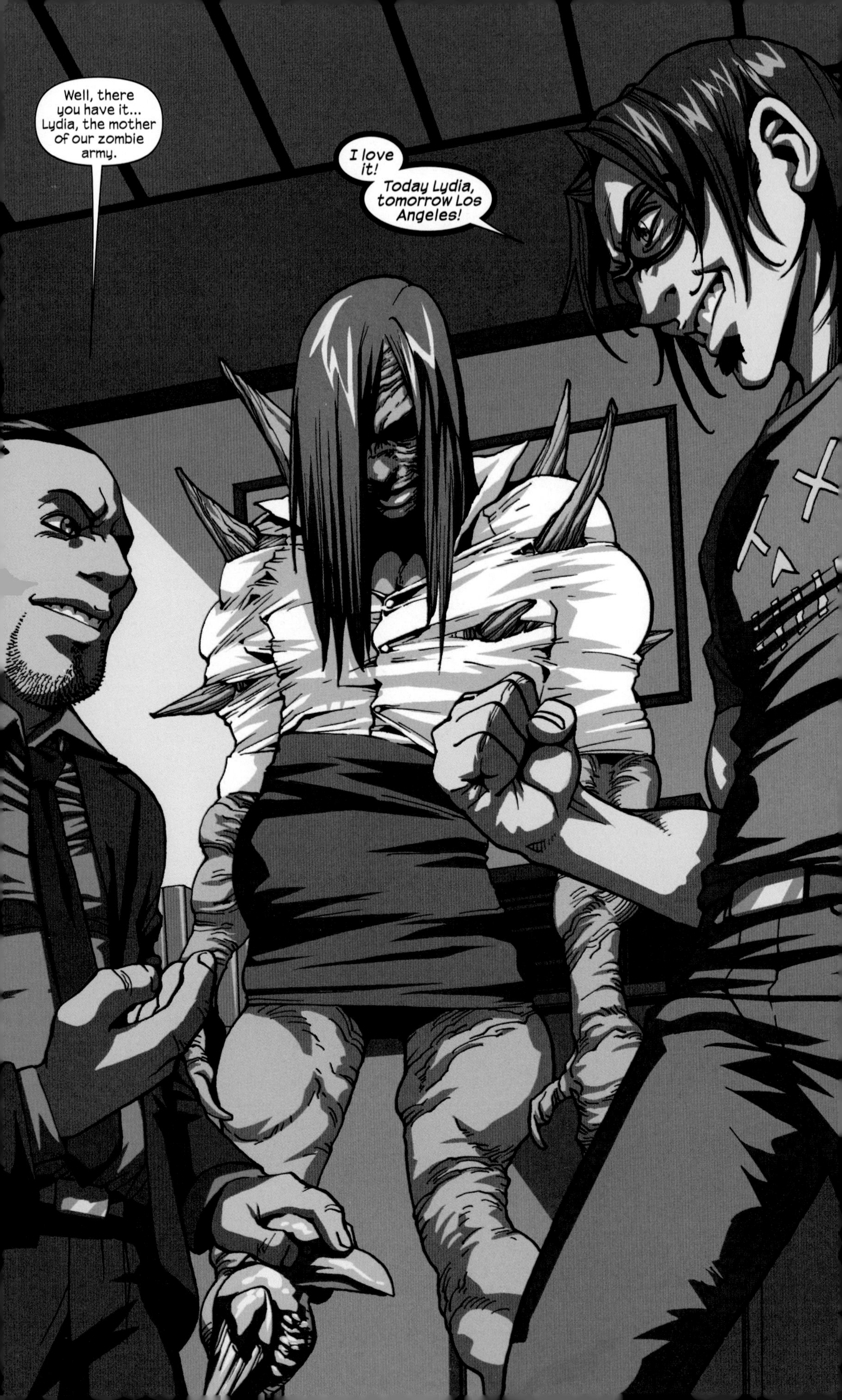
Well, there you have it... Lydia, the mother of our zombie army.
I love it!
Today Lydia, tomorrow Los Angeles!

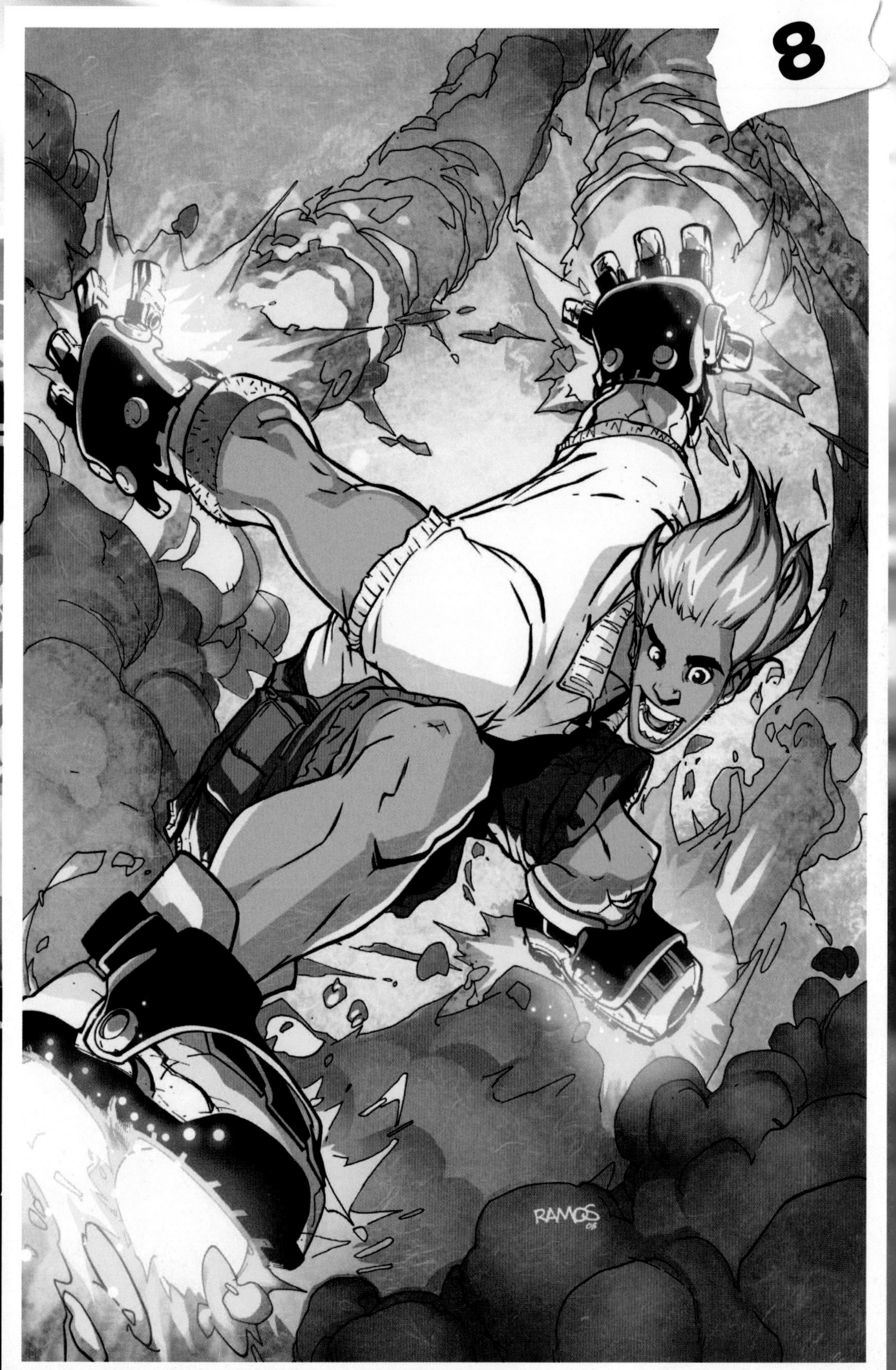
8
RAMOS

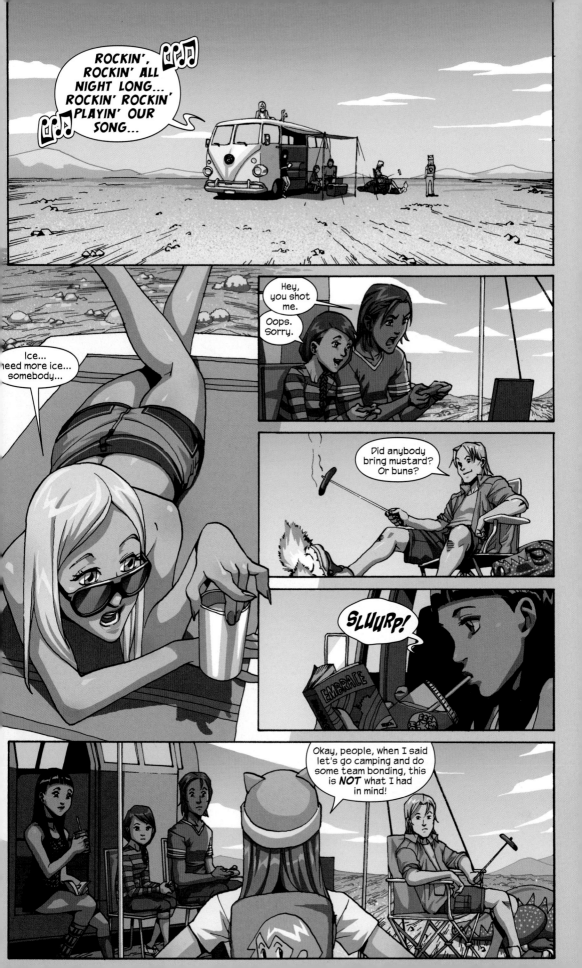

Everybody listen up! This is a *camp-out!* Turn off all electronic devices **EEE-MEEDIATELY!**

Chase, put that footstigon in the bus.

Klara, stop shooting Victor!

Victor, turn off that laptop!

Nico, close that book!

Karolina... put some clothes on!

Fine. Sun's going down anyway.

Since when did we start letting the kid boss us around?

She's got a point. Here we are. We might as well make the most of it.

When we get our fire built, I have a surprise for you guys...

Costume designs!

Groan!

Molly...

So where are we supposed to find firewood in the desert?

Really? We're getting costumes?

Can we have petticoats?

Wow!

You get a cape made of rose petals.

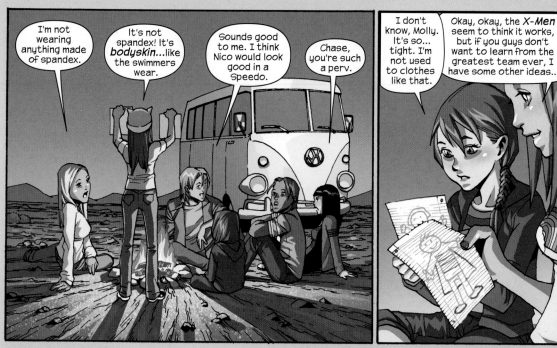

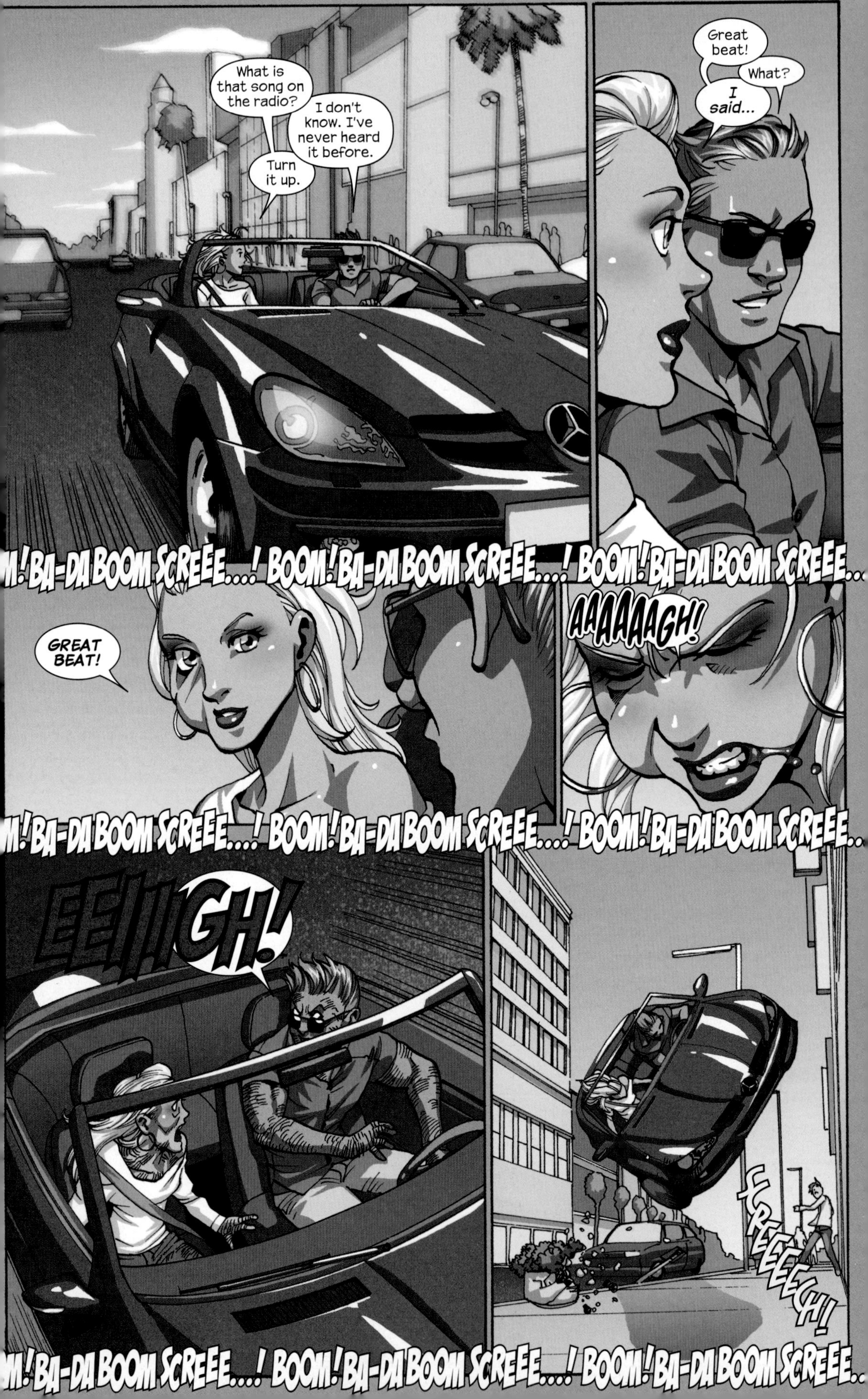

What is that song on the radio?
I don't know. I've never heard it before.
Turn it up.
Great beat!
What?
I said...
M! BA-DA BOOM SCREEE...! BOOM! BA-DA BOOM SCREEE...! BOOM! BA-DA BOOM SCREEE...
GREAT BEAT!
AAAAAAGH!
M! BA-DA BOOM SCREEE...! BOOM! BA-DA BOOM SCREEE...! BOOM! BA-DA BOOM SCREEE...
EEIIIGH!
SCREEEECH!
M! BA-DA BOOM SCREEE...! BOOM! BA-DA BOOM SCREEE...! BOOM! BA-DA BOOM SCREEE...

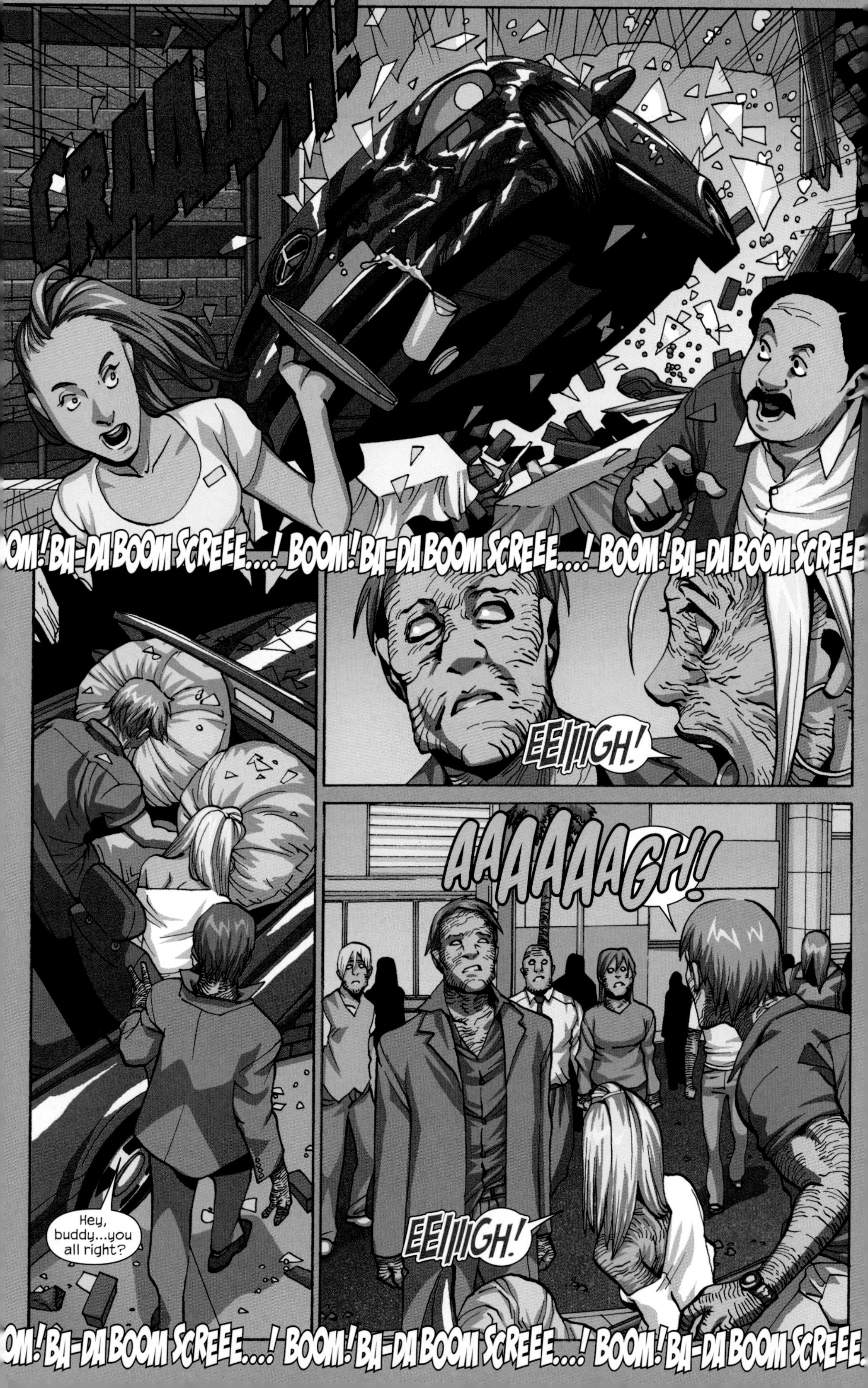
CRAAASH!
OM! BA-DA BOOM SCREEE...! BOOM! BA-DA BOOM SCREEE...! BOOM! BA-DA BOOM SCREEE
EEIIIIGH!
Hey, buddy...you all right?
AAAAAAGH!
EEIIIIGH!
OM! BA-DA BOOM SCREEE...! BOOM! BA-DA BOOM SCREEE...! BOOM! BA-DA BOOM SCREEE.

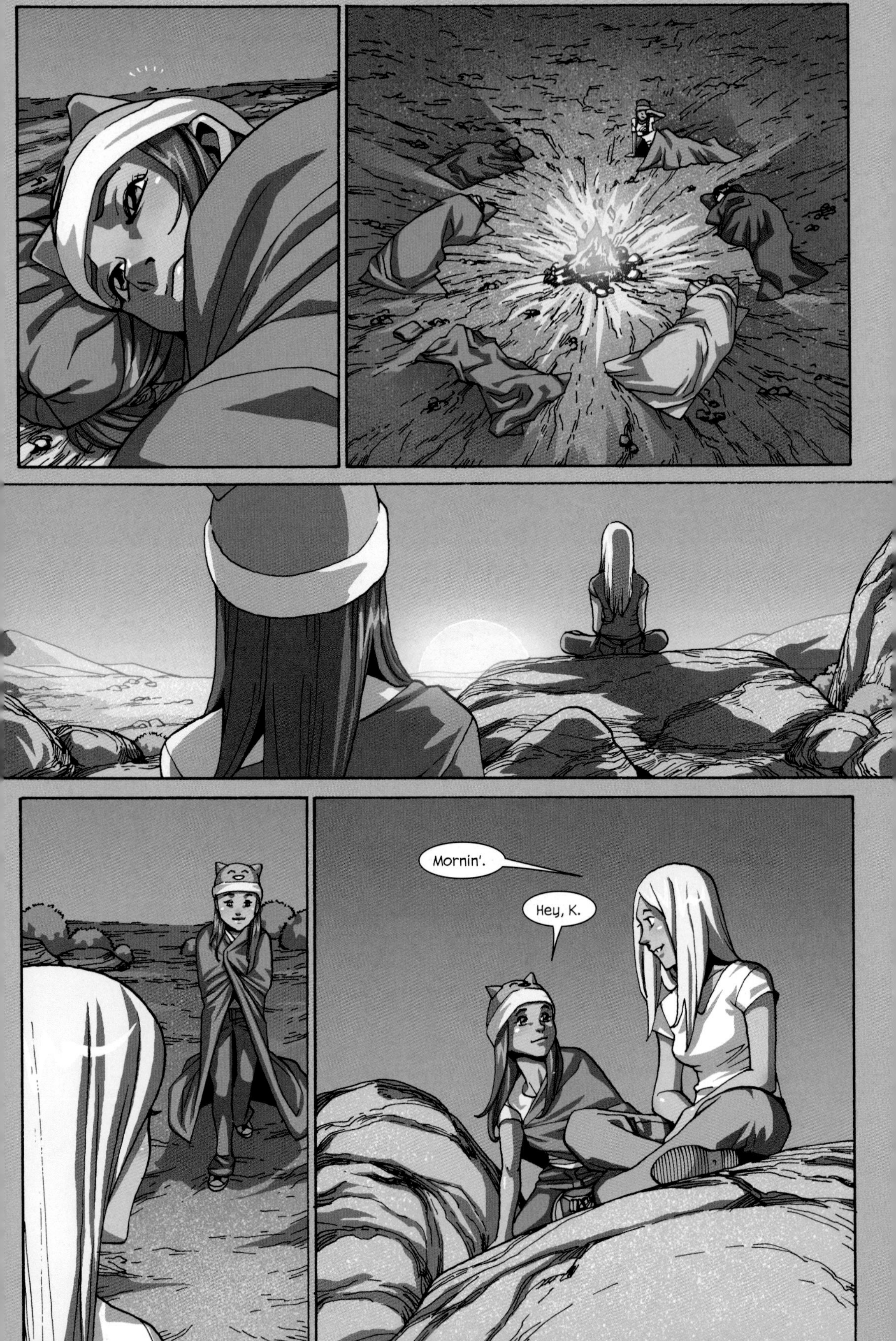

Mornin'.
Hey, K.

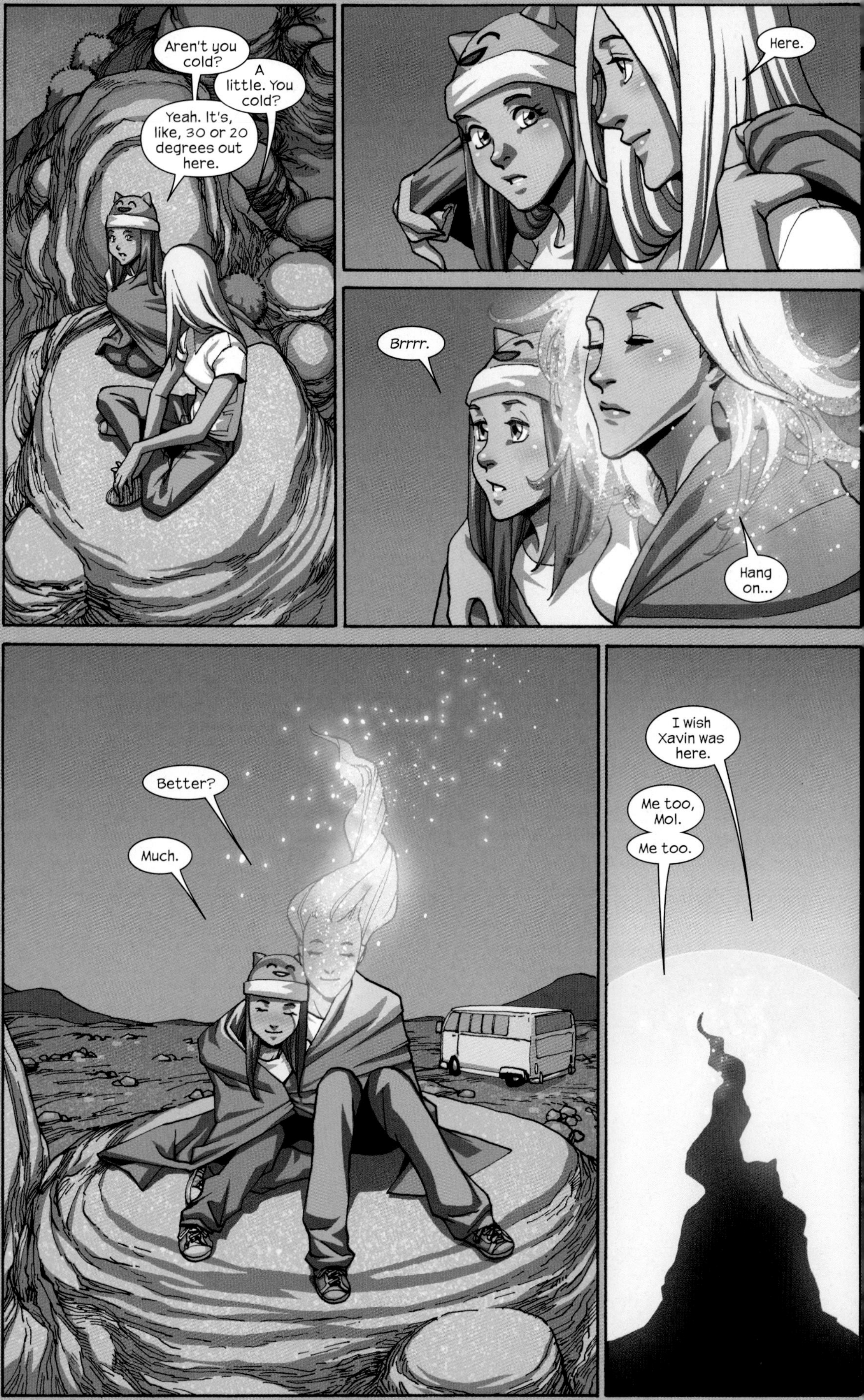
Aren't you cold?
A little. You cold?
Yeah. It's, like, 30 or 20 degrees out here.
Here.
Brrrr.
Hang on...
Better?
Much.
I wish Xavin was here.
Me too, Mol.
Me too.

OOM! BA-DA BOOM SCREEE....! BOOM! BA-DA BOOM SCREEE....! BOOM! BA-DA BOOM SCREE

OOM! BA-DA BOOM SCREEE....! BOOM! BA-DA BOOM SCREEE....! BOOM! BA-DA BOOM SCREE

Okay. Now what?

Nico, you said you heard a spell in the song. If magic turned these people into zombies, can you reverse it?

I don't think so. I can't even reverse my own spells.

It's easy. Just get out your stick and say Unzombie!

We better do something, because if they get any closer all bets are off on that peace and love crap.

Nico...? You want me to get us out of here my way?

Karolina, get the girls out of harm's way.

Check.

Hey...!

Nicooo... no more Mr. Nice Guy!

When Blood Is Shed, Let The Staff Of One Emerge!

SMACK!

Sorry, guys, time to act!

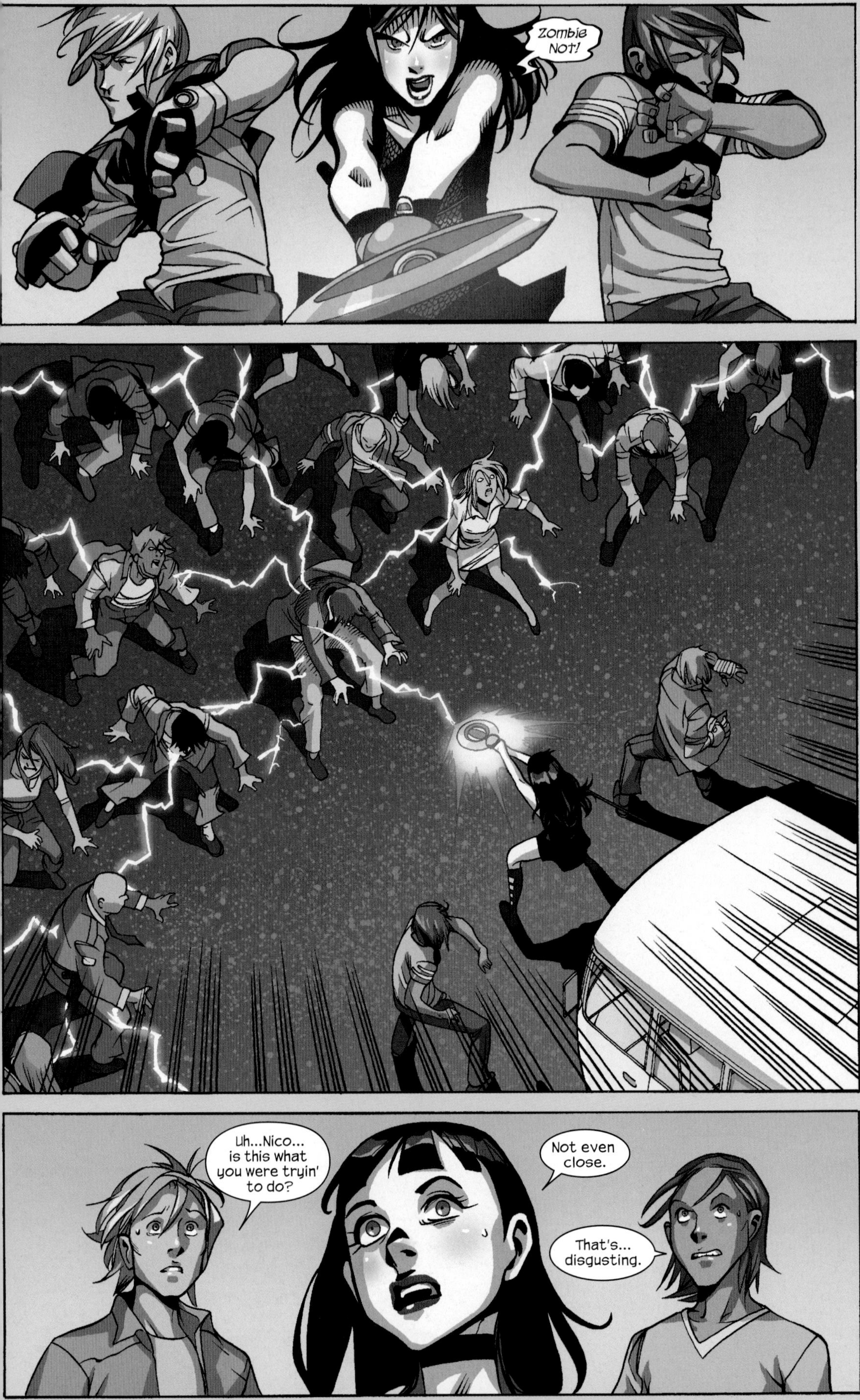
Zombie Not!
Uh...Nico... is this what you were tryin' to do?
Not even close.
That's... disgusting.

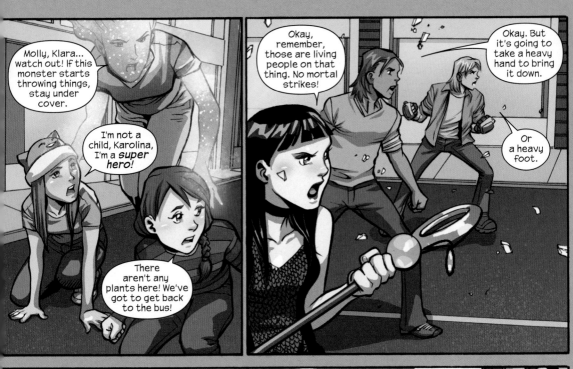

What was **THAT?!**

I'm still working on my aim! Gimme a break!

Let me show you how it's done, Bullseye.

**SNAP!**

**KRAACK!**

**BOOM!**

Whoa! A little *warning* next time!

**POP!**

**POW!**

**KRACK!**

**POW!**

Wow! Awesome job, Super-Fart! Can I have your autograph?

Yeah, and you know where you can put it.

Let's see if a little juice will split them up.

SHOOARGHSH! SHOOARGHSH!

FAUGHOOOW!

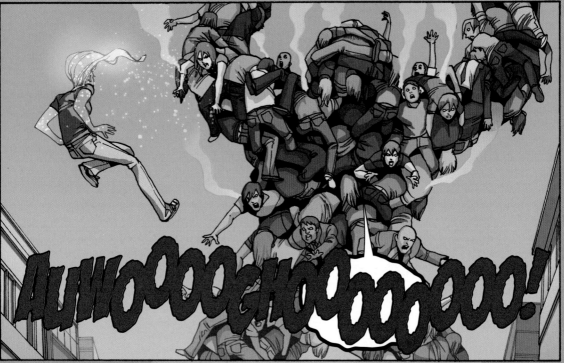

AUWOOOOOGHOOOOOOOO!

Eww, that's GROSS!!

My rose! Gotta get my rose!

Oily!

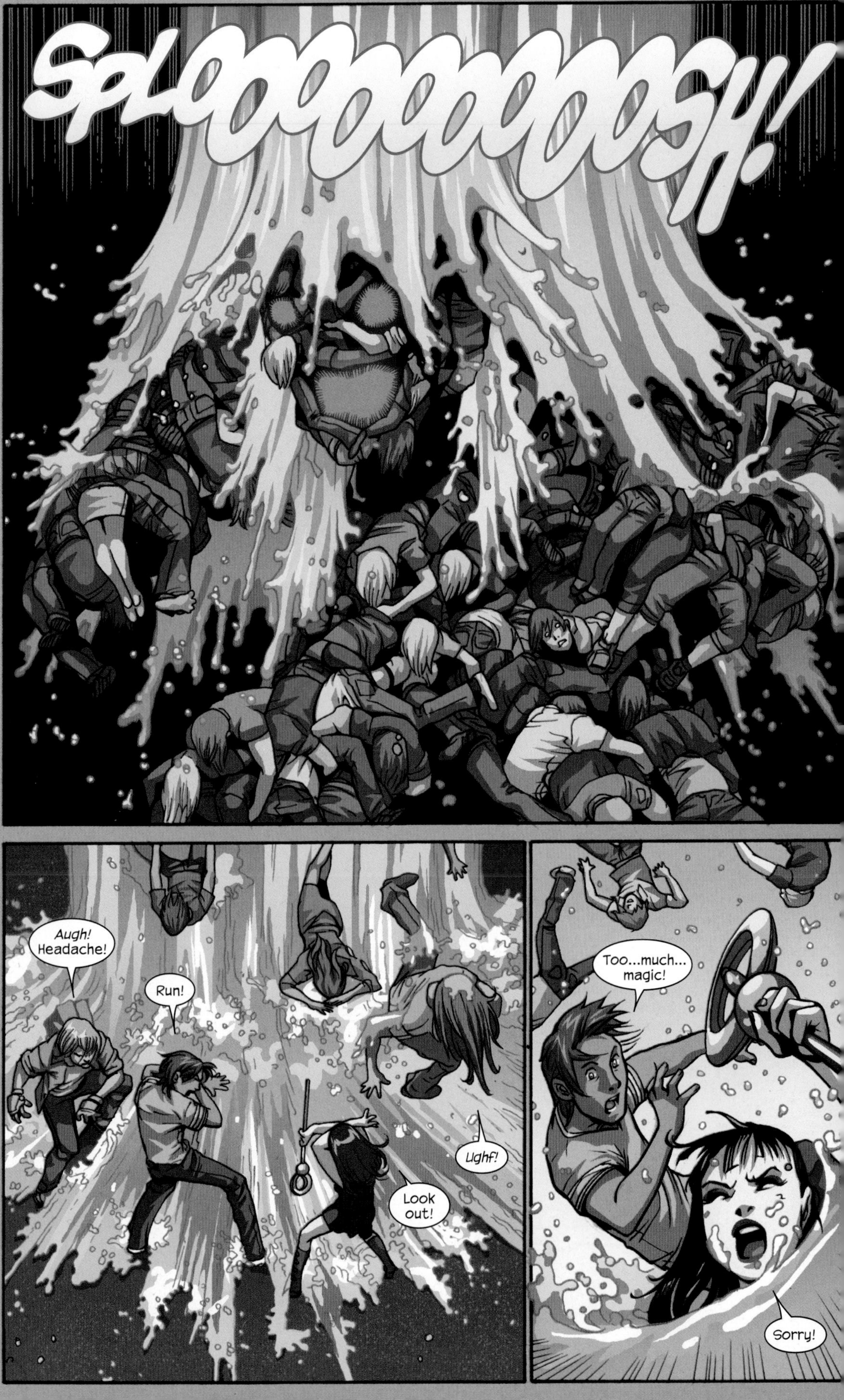
SPLOOOOOOOOSH!
Augh! Headache!
Run!
Ughf!
Look out!
Too...much... magic!
Sorry!

I'm sorry, guys. I don't know what's going on with my magic. The scatter spell, that creature... the oil. Everything I try is like way too much.

Maybe you're getting stronger. Do you feel stronger?

I'm not sure what I feel. I think...I don't know. Ever since my great-grandmother tortured me...

She *tortured* you?! Your own great-grand-mother?!

I told you that. She was trying to make me stronger. You were just too distracted by Lily to notice anything else.

*Oof!*

Let's don't go over that again. I remember. It just sounded odd to hear you say it like that.

That's what it is, Nico. Your great-grandmother did something to you. To your powers.

I'm okay... if anybody cares.

So, before we were so rudely interrupted...

To the radio station.

Yes.

The one in the *mall?* We're going to the *mall?! Yay!*

**Help!** Help, somebody!

Chase!

Chase? Where are you?

In here. Val's office!

Oh my gosh!

Lydia? Lydia...talk to me, okay? Tell me what's goin' on.

AUGHHHHHHHH!

I know her. She works here. She's hot. Or she was. Don't let her jump!

HOOOTWW.

Lydia? Lydia, can you hear me?

We're here to help you.

AGHGULIE

I've heard enough. Lock off all exits and move in with caution.

Ah, the sound of sirens. Did anybody invite the cops? *NO!* Are we going to let them spoil our right to congregate? *NO!*

*STOP THE COPS! STOP THE COPS! ZOMBIES FIGHT AND STOP THE COPS!*

*Heard enough?*

More than enough. Everybody to the exits. Stop the cops and zombies from clashing before somebody gets hurt.

Where are you going?

I'm going to see a man about a spell.

Shame on you, Val Rhymin! What you have done to these people is a crime!

What the hell...?

Mother of Magic! *The Staff of One!*

And **you!** Keep your hands where I can see them!

Get her! She's just a girl, you idiots. **Get her!**

AAARRGH!

COCOON!

Just a girl. Famous last words. Say hello to a girl of prey.

KREEEEE!

Now... as I was saying...

It's **you!** You're the one!

The one?

You're **the Minoru girl!**

At last...The sacred Staff Of One is *mine!* All the power of the past, present and future at my beck and call! I am unstoppable! I am....

WWIIGHHHHHH!

AAIGH!

HELP! HELP! AIIIGH!

KREAUURRRGH!

KREAUURRRGH!

WHISSSSH!

KLUINK! KINK!

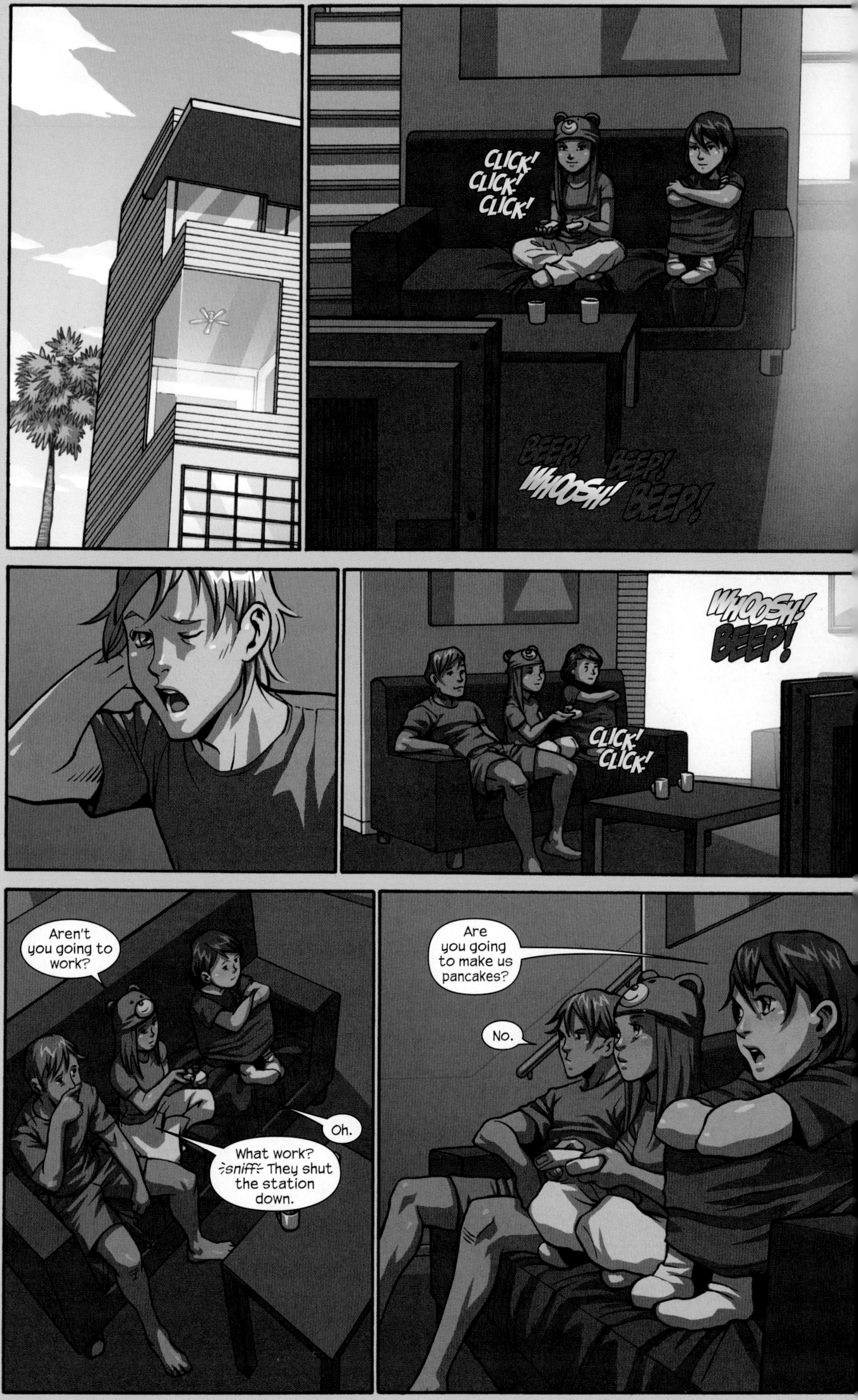
CLICK! CLICK! CLICK!
BEEP! WHOOSH! BEEP! BEEP!
WHOOSH! BEEP!
CLICK! CLICK!
Aren't you going to work?
What work? ~sniff~ They shut the station down.
Oh.
Are you going to make us pancakes?
No.

Me either.

You girls did good yesterday.

Thanks. I wasn't scared once.

CLICK! CLICK! CLICK!

BEEP! WHOOSH! BEEP! BEEP!

You girls are the future of super heroes. You know that?

Yep.

Mm-hmm.

CLICK! CLICK! CLICK!

BEEP! WHOOSH! BEEP! BEEP!

CLICK! CLICK! CLICK!

BEEP! WHOOSH! BEEP! BEEP!

THE END

10

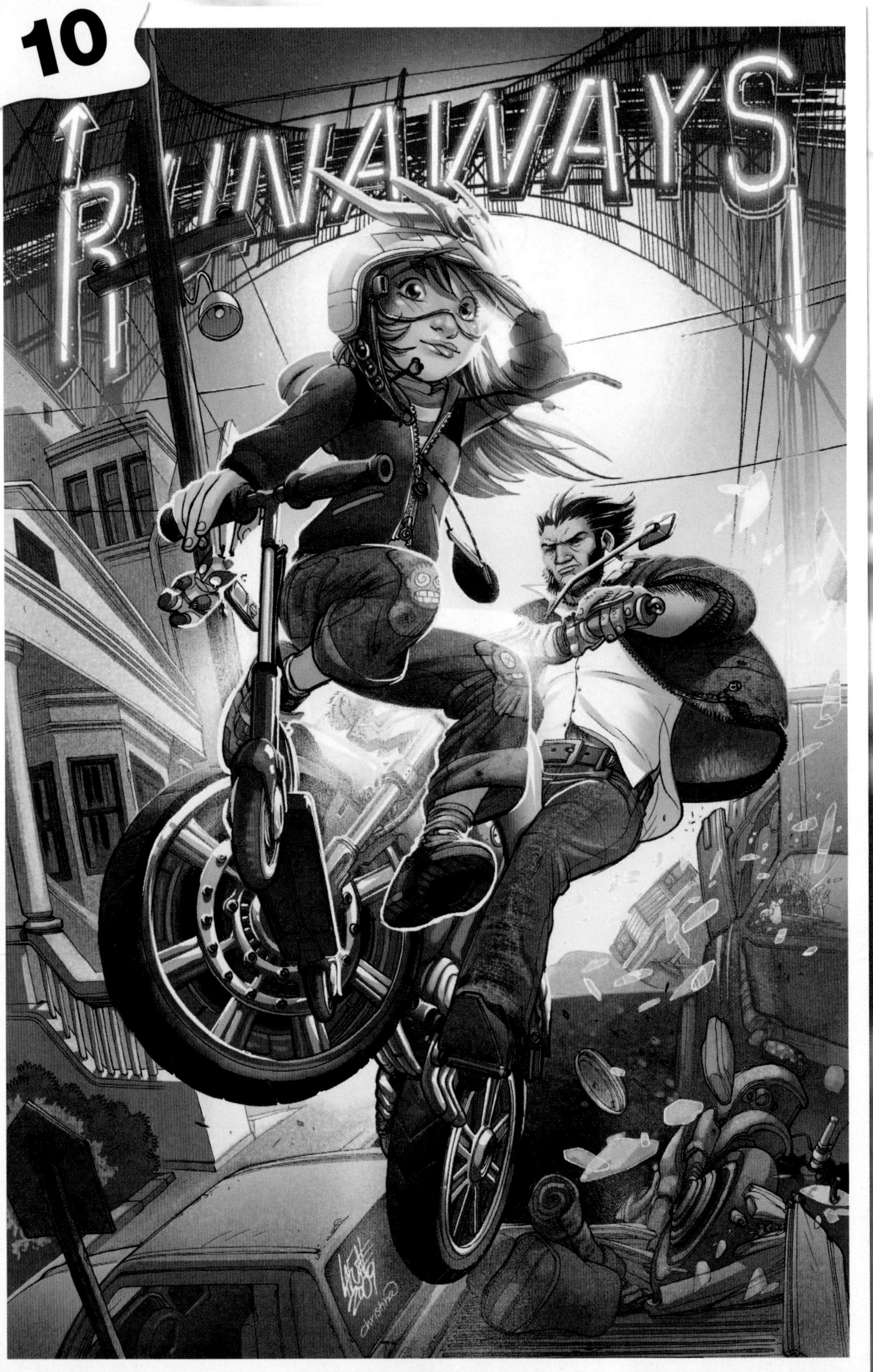

Dear Lord...

Anderson to command...

We've got a situation.

They're... they're all *dead*...

Sir, what the hell happened here?

Look at all this... this armor, this much firepower...these guys could have taken over Los Angeles.

Are...are these super-villains?

I've got a live one over here!!

Geez... look at the poor bastard. Whatever happened...he saw it all.

Sir... what could have done this?

SAN FRANCISCO, 98 MILES PER HOUR.

So we have to make a stop... I'm gonna go get this special *sword*, and I need you to cut off my *head* with it.

No. And that's *gross*.

Your parents were all super-villains, is that it? You gotta be kidding me.

I mean, what the hell kind of super-villains raised *you*? Evil Care Bears? My Little Evil Pony?

Don't you talk about my mom and dad!

You woulda been better off if they made *you* evil, too. At least then you'd have a better picture of how the world actually works, 'cuz right now--

SNFF!

Are...are you smelling me?

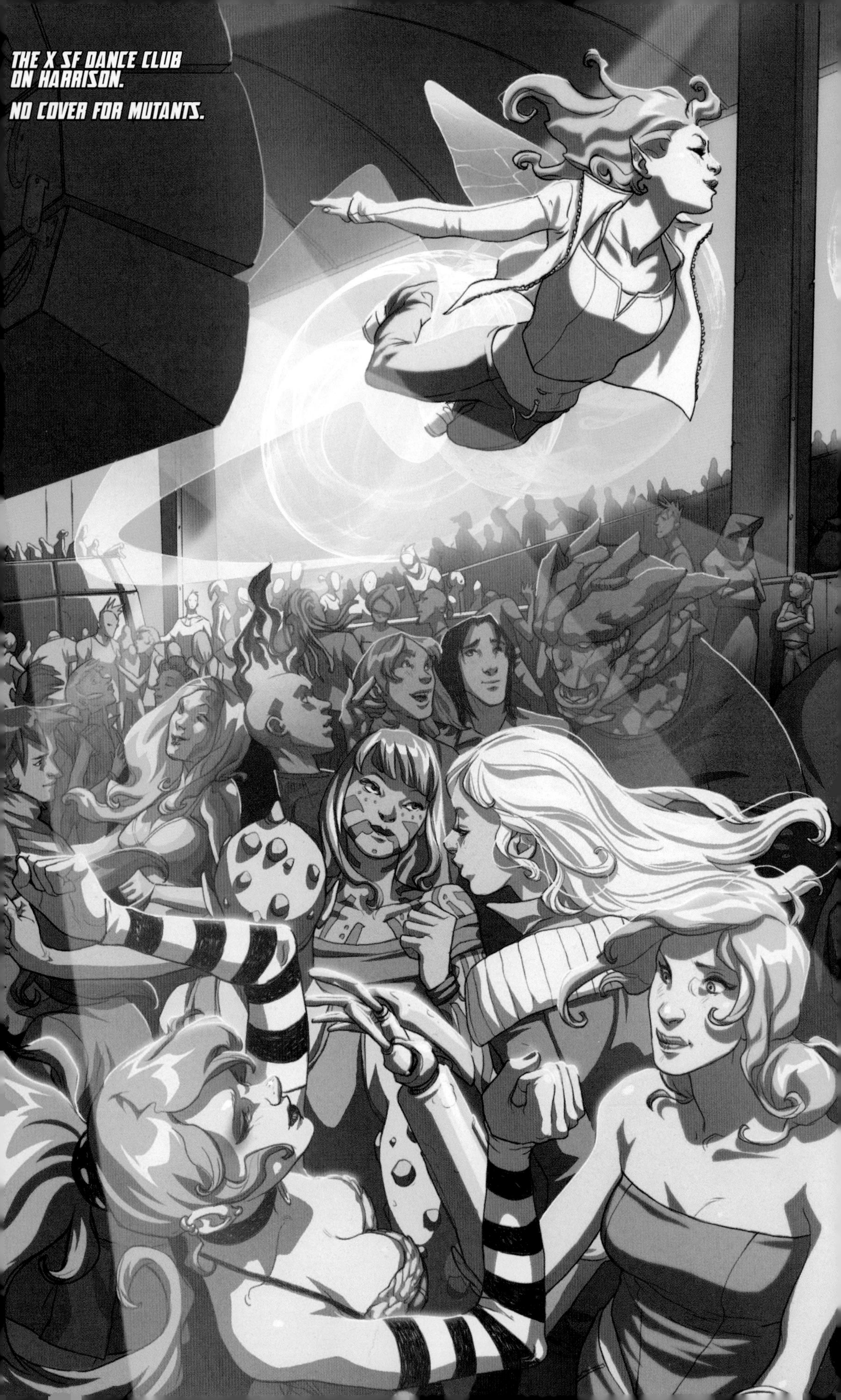
THE X SF DANCE CLUB
ON HARRISON.
NO COVER FOR MUTANTS.

*Hnnn... I'm awake, mom...I'm...*

...hey. Are we back in the Danger Room?

Because this seems a lot more dangerous.

Just don't freak out, Hayes. I'll handle this.

This is *your* fault, isn't it?! Someone tried to blow me up because I was with *you!*

Man! Nobody likes you, do they?

You're wrong, Miss Hayes...we didn't come for *him.*

We came for *you.* It took me a *year* to find you, but now I'm finally going to have revenge on the Outcasts.

Your *parents.*

You knew my parents?! Were you friends? I don't remember seeing you in any of our pictures, but maybe--

FRIENDS?! Do you even know who your parents *were*, girl?

I...I know. They... they were super-villains.

Oh, no. They weren't super-villains, you little &$#@%. *I'm* a super-villain. What they were was *far* worse.

"My crew and I were going to make a play for a chunk of the Pride's territory."

"Your parents killed them all. Right in front of me. They did something to me...I had to watch. I couldn't stop *watching*."

"Whatever they did to me, I couldn't move...I couldn't talk...they had to put drops in my *eyes* to keep them moist because I couldn't *shut them*.

"I couldn't close my eyes to *sleep*. I almost went *insane*...but then it stopped."

After *seven years*, it stopped!

SEVEN YEARS!!

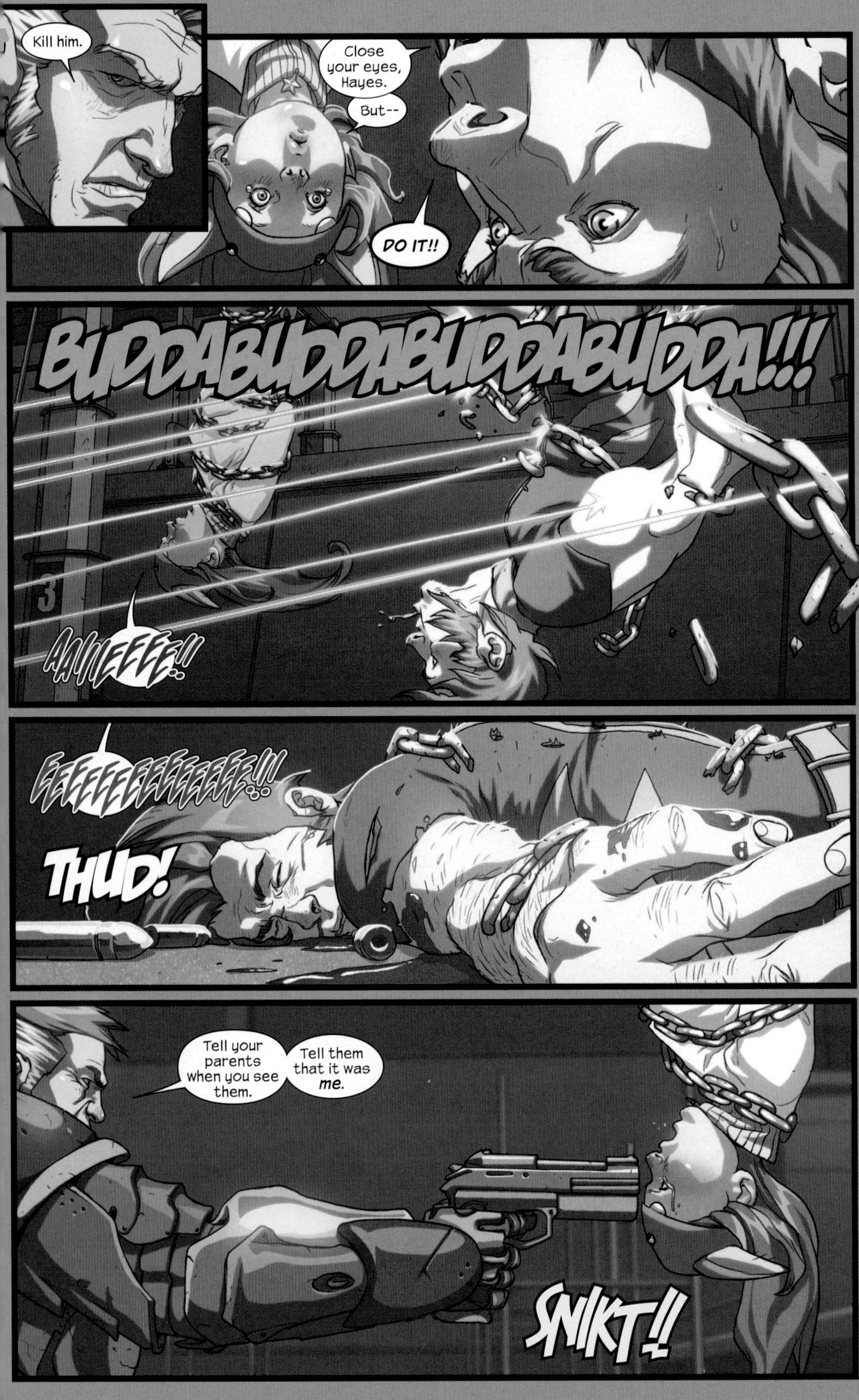

Kill him.
Close your eyes, Hayes.
But--
DO IT!!
BUDDABUDDABUDDABUDDA!!!
AAIIEEEE!!
EEEEEEEEEEEEEE!!!
THUD!
Tell your parents when you see them.
Tell them that it was *me*.
SNIKT!!

UHNNN!!

THUNK!!

SNIKT!!

YOU WANNA TALK TO PEOPLE IN HELL? GET READY!

NO!

Super-villains kill. Not super heroes.

You're a super hero.

Not like my parents.

Kid...

I'm sorry your parents are dead, girl.

Sorry I couldn't kill them *myself*.

LATER.

"I want to go home now."

Mol...I know we were kind of down on the X-Men before, but you should really give them another try.

They're so *nice!* The students were so much fun, you're going to *love* it!

Seriously, Mol...you should--

THIS PLACE IS HORRIBLE AND YOU ARE TAKING ME HOME RIGHT NOW OR I WILL BEAT YOU ALL UP FOREVER!

Are you sure you don't want to--

JUST DRIVE!!

END.

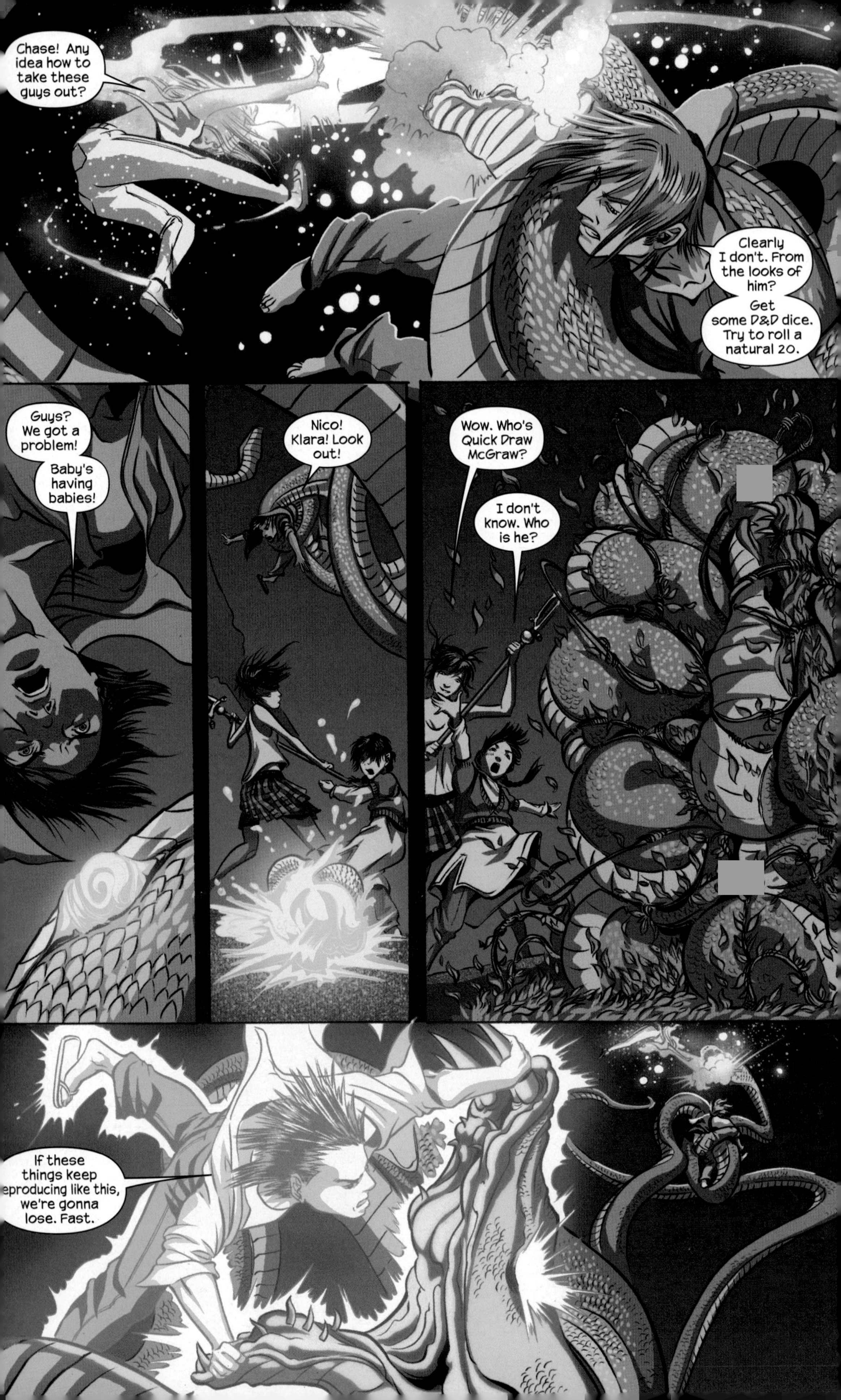

Chase! Any idea how to take these guys out?
Clearly I don't. From the looks of him?
Get some D&D dice. Try to roll a natural 20.
Guys? We got a problem!
Baby's having babies!
Nico! Klara! Look out!
Wow. Who's Quick Draw McGraw?
I don't know. Who is he?
If these things keep eproducing like this, we're gonna lose. Fast.

THE END.

9
VARIANT BY
DAVID LAFUENTE

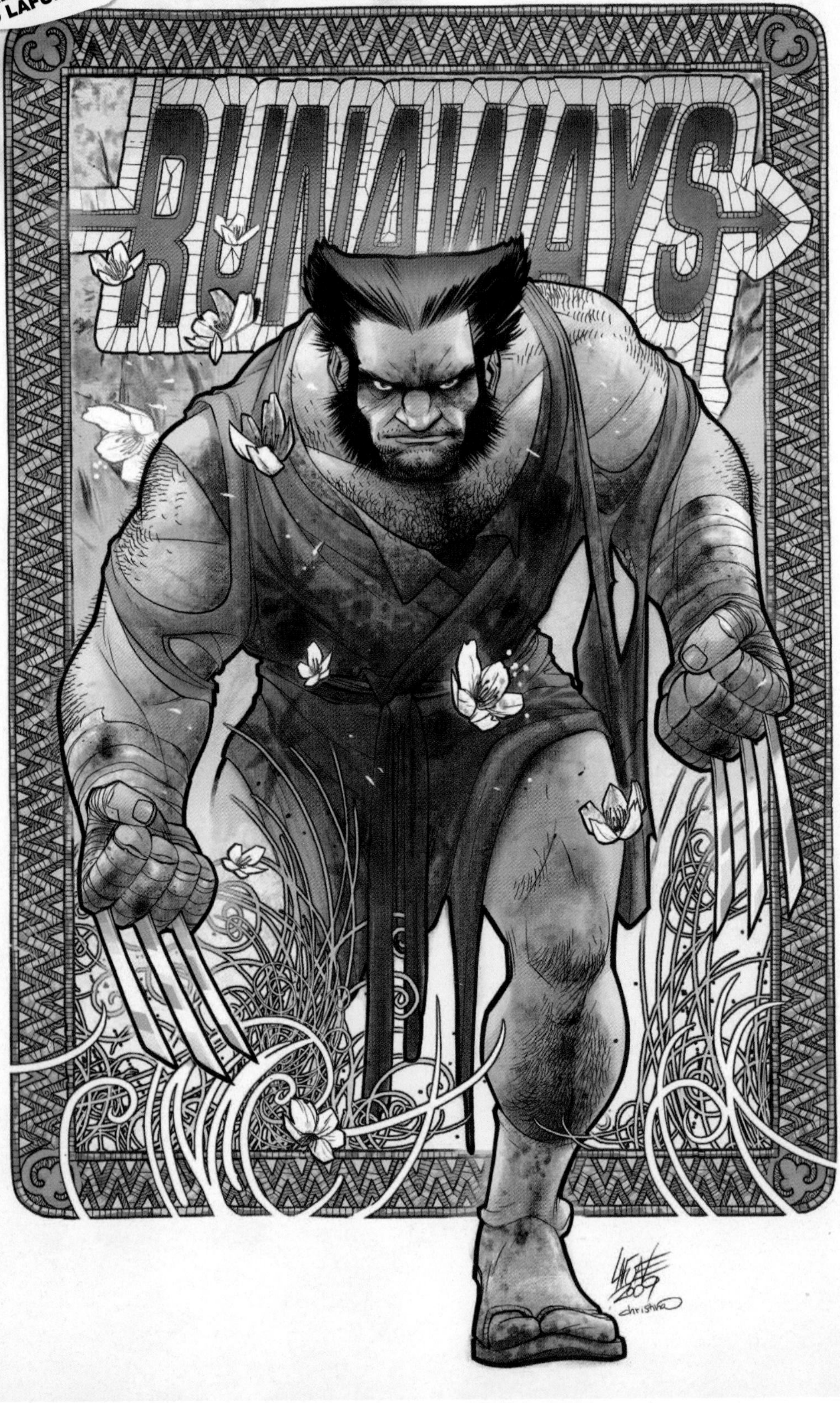
RUNAWAYS

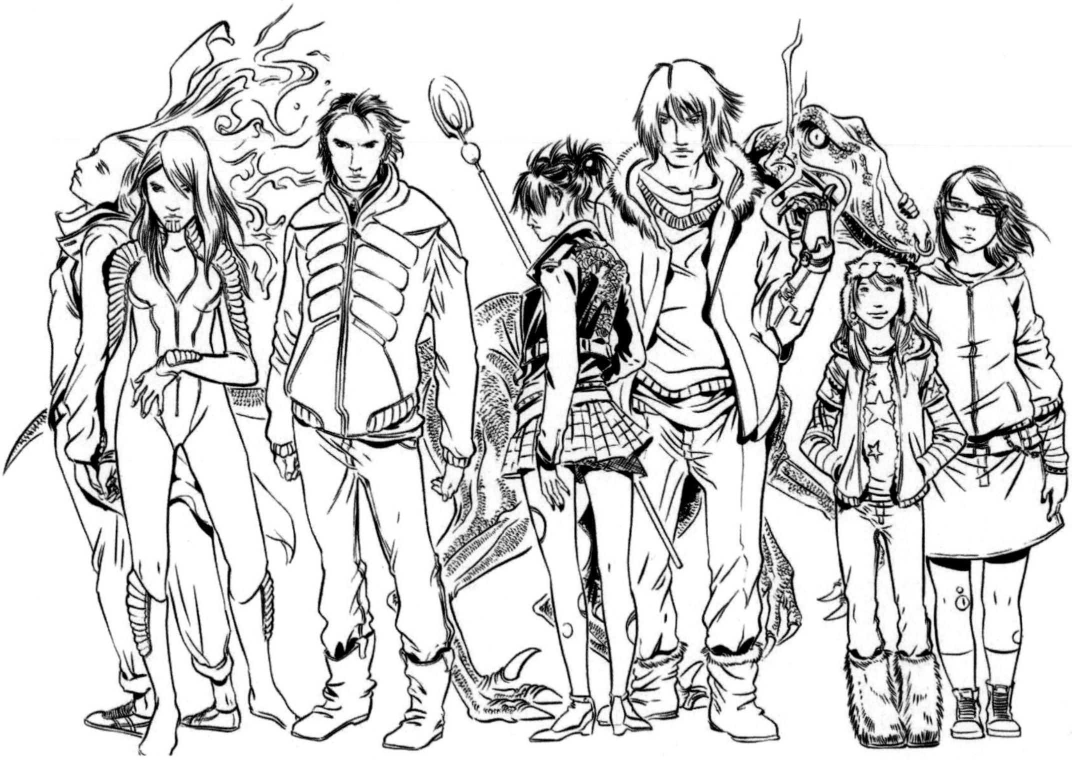

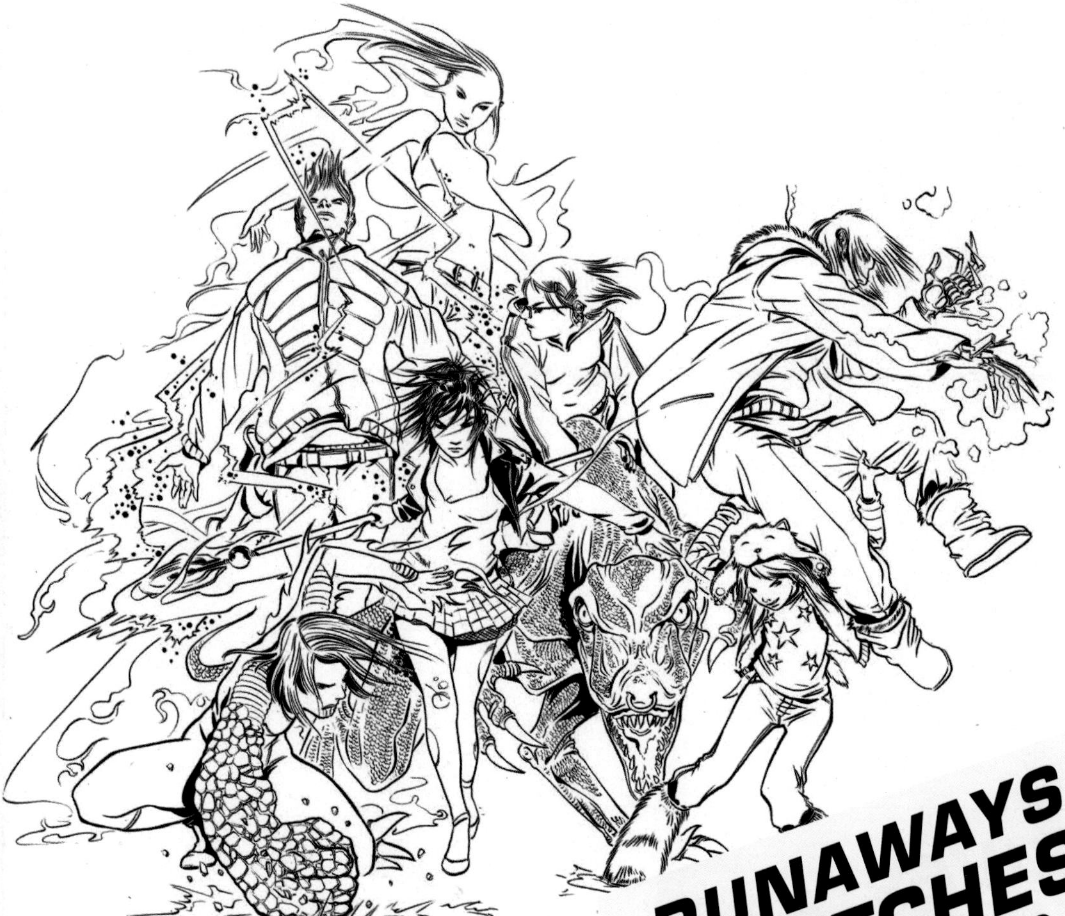

# RUNAWAYS SKETCHES
BY EMMA RIOS

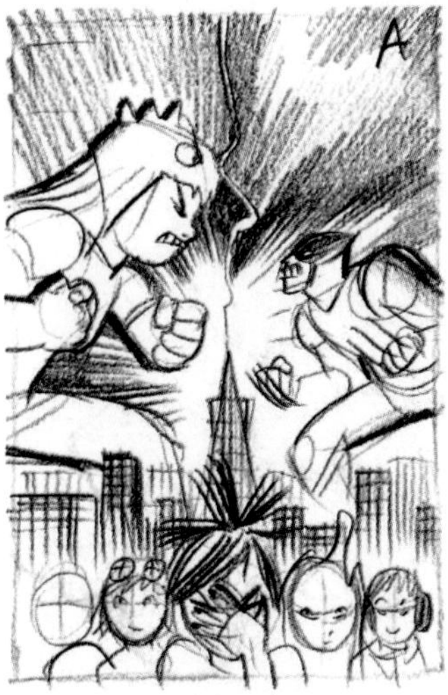
A

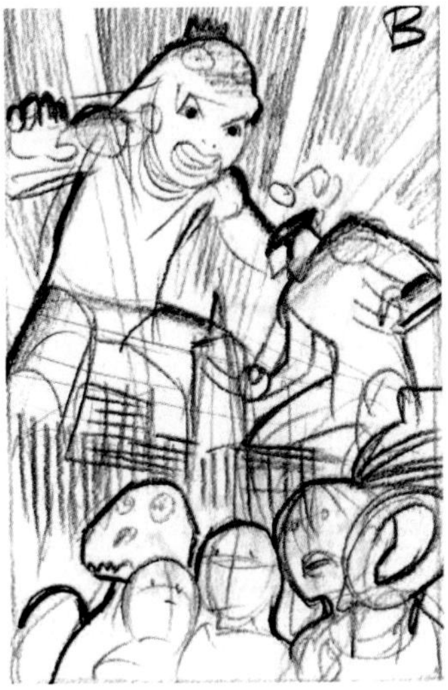
B

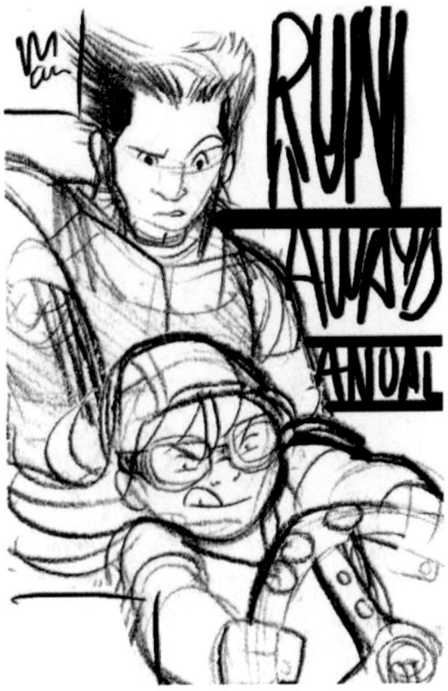
RUN

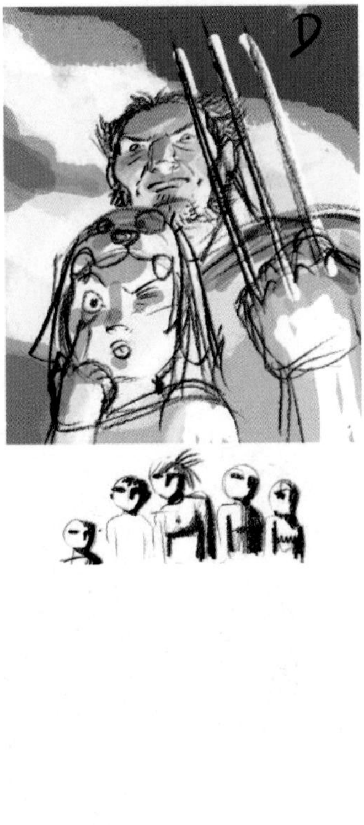
D

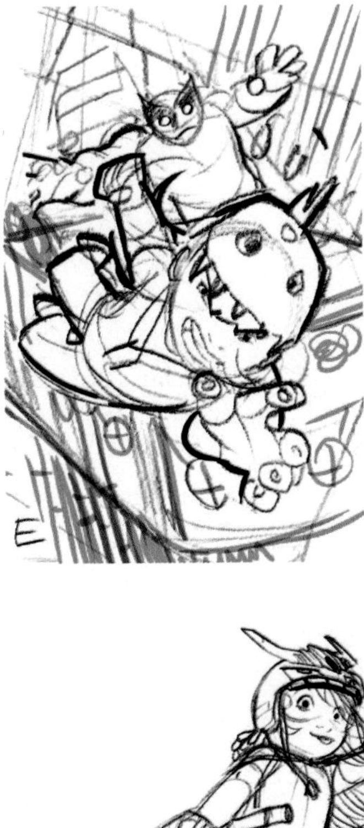
E

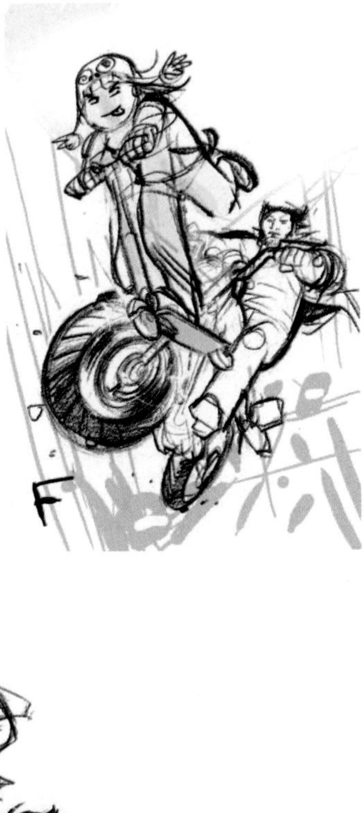
F

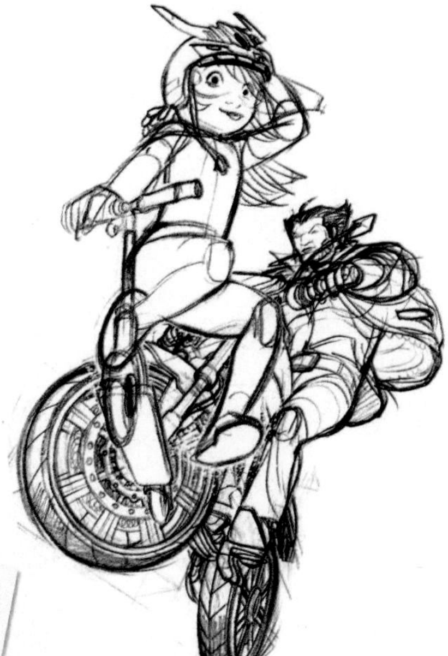

# COVER #10 PROCESS

BY DAVID LAFUENTE

INKS

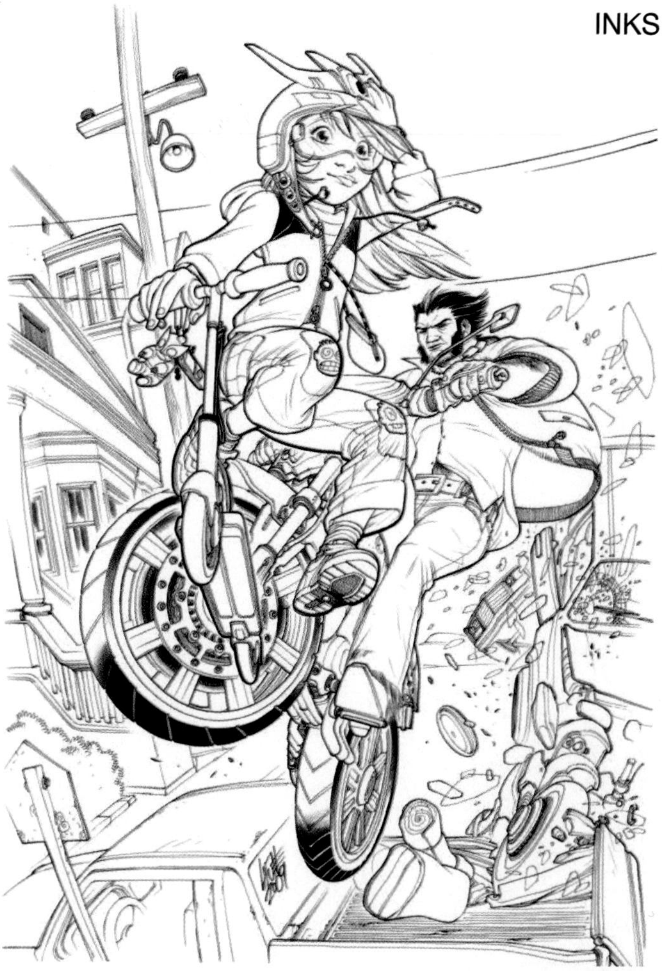

ALTERNATE COLORS

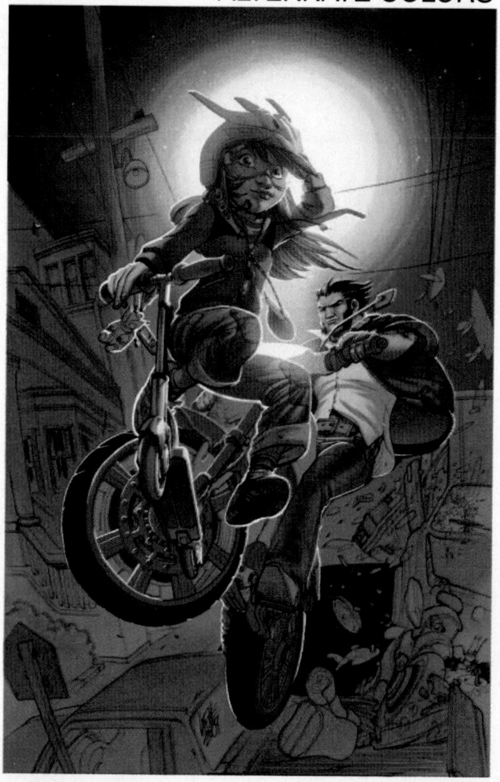

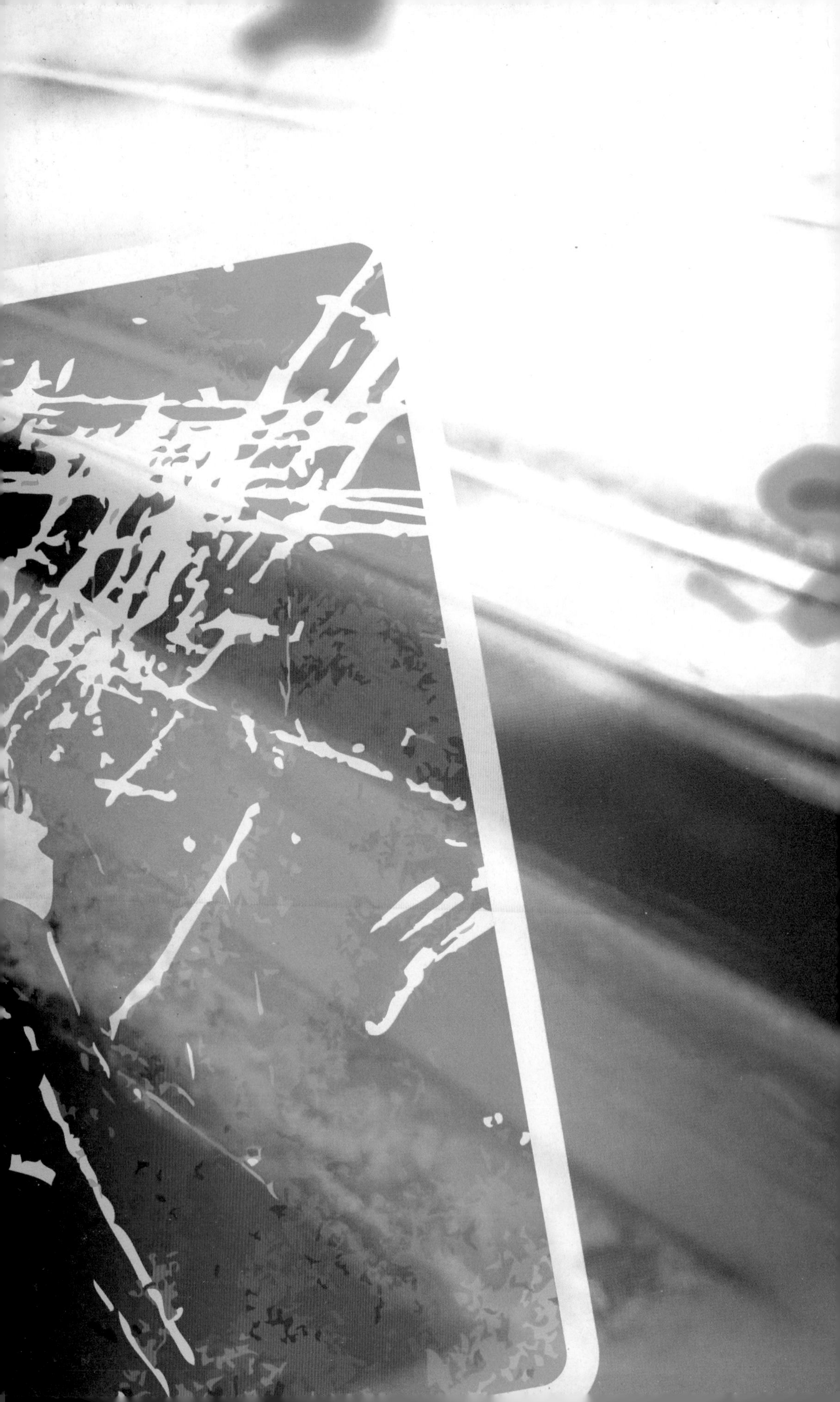